Netv ... ...

The "*How to*" Made Simple

A Desktop Quick Reference

Network Documentation
The "*How to*" Made Simple
A Desktop Quick Reference

Kurtis G. Kent

Etapmus Press

Texas, USA

Network Documentation

The "*How to*" Made Simple
By
Kurtis G. Kent

Published by Etapmus Press, 1011 San Antonio, Forney, TX 75126.

Etapmus Press books may be purchased for educational, business, or sales promotional use. Online editions may also be available. For more information, contact Etapmus Press by visiting our website *www.etapmuspress.com,* or contact our Institutional/corporate sales department at *bookorders@etapmusspress.com.*

Printing History:
February 2010:   First Edition

Printed in USA by 48HrBooks (www.48HrBooks.com)
ISBN (978-0-9832775-0-7)

Contents

ACKNOWLEDGEMENTS 9

INTRODUCTION 11

    DO I NEED THIS BOOK? 11
    HOW ITS ORGANIZED 15
    THE HIDDEN VALUE 16

CHAPTER 1 - GETTING PREPARED 19

    BASIC NETWORK DIAGRAM 22
    INVENTORY LIST 25

CHAPTER 2 – BASIC INFORMATION 29

    CONTACT LIST 29
    SITE LOCATION INFORMATION 33
    NETWORK OVERVIEW 35
    NETWORK DIAGRAM 38
    NETWORK ENVIRONMENT 39

CHAPTER 3 – INTERNET & TELCO 43

    INTERNET DOMAIN REGISTRATION INFORMATION 43
    DOMAIN REGISTRATION INFORMATION 45
    PUBLIC DNS HOST RECORD SHEET 47
    INTERNET SERVICE PROVIDER INFORMATION 48
    TELCO PROVIDER INFORMATION 50
    ROUTER CONFIGURATION 52

CHAPTER 4 - NETWORK SECURITY 55

    PASSWORD POLICY 55
    GROUP POLICIES 57
    NETWORK PASSWORDS 60
    FIREWALL CONFIGURATION 61

CHAPTER 5 – NETWORK INFORMATION 67

    NETWORK QUICK REFERENCE 67
    CONTRACTS, WARRANTIES AND LICENSE INFORMATION 69
    SOFTWARE LICENSE & INSTALL KEY INFORMATION 71
    KEY DEVICE INFORMATION 73
    PRINTER INFORMATION 75
    KVM SWITCH INFORMATION 79
    COMPUTER SUMMARY DETAILS 81

CHAPTER 6 – NETWORK AND DOMAIN 85

    FILE AND PRINT SHARES.. 85
    WINS 88

DHCP 89
DNS 90
ACTIVE DIRECTORY DOMAIN INFORMATION 92
SERVER ROLES 95
MS SQL DATABASE INFORMATION 97
EMAIL CONFIGURATION 99
BACKUP INFORMATION 104

APPENDIX **107**

LOGIN SCRIPTS 108
FORMS AND TEMPLATES 110
THE BOOK TABS 111

Diagrams & Forms

FIGURE 1 - BASIC NETWORK DIAGRAM 22
FIGURE 2 - INVENTORY LIST TEMPLATE 25
FIGURE 3 - INVENTORY LIST EXAMPLE 26
FIGURE 4 - ADVANCED INVENTORY LIST TEMPLATE 27
FIGURE 5- INTERNAL CONTACTS 29
FIGURE 6 - ESCALATION LIST 30
FIGURE 7 - VENDOR TECH SUPPORT 31
FIGURE 8 - TELCO CONTACT LIST 32
FIGURE 9 – SITE LOCATION INFORMATION 34
FIGURE 10 – EXAMPLE NETWORK DIAGRAM 38
FIGURE 11 – DOMAIN NAME REGISTRATION FORM 46
FIGURE 12 – PUBLIC DNS HOST FORM 47
FIGURE 13 – EXAMPLE INTERNET SERVICE PROVIDER FORM 49
FIGURE 14 – EXAMPLE ISP SITE ADDRESS INFORMATION 49
FIGURE 15 – EXAMPLE TELCO PROVIDER FORM 51
FIGURE 16 – EXAMPLE TELCO SITE ADDRESS INFORMATION 51
FIGURE 17 – ROUTER CONFIGURATION FORM 54
FIGURE 18 – NETWORK SECURITY BASIC FORM 59
FIGURE 19 – EXAMPLE NETWORK PASSWORD FORM 61
FIGURE 20 – FIREWALL CONFIGURATION FORM 66
FIGURE 21 – NETWORK QUICK REFERENCE EXAMPLE 68
FIGURE 22 –EXAMPLE CONTRACTS, & LICENSE INFORMATION 70
FIGURE 23 – SOFTWARE LICENSE & KEY INFORMATION 72
FIGURE 24 – KEY DEVICE INFORMATION FORM 74
FIGURE 25 – PRINTER INFORMATION FORM 76
FIGURE 26 – PDU DEVICE INFORMATION FORM 78
FIGURE 27 – KVM DEVICE INFORMATION FORM 80
FIGURE 28 – COMPUTER DETAILS FORM 83
FIGURE 29 – PC SUMMARY TABLE FORM 84
FIGURE 30 – FILE & PRINT SHARE FORM 87
FIGURE 31 – WINS FORM 88
FIGURE 32 – DHCP FORM 89
FIGURE 33 – DNS INFORMATION FORM 90
FIGURE 34 – DNS HOST RECORDS FORM 91
FIGURE 35 – KEY ACTIVE DIRECTORY COMPONENTS 94
FIGURE 36 – KEY SERVER ROLES FORM 96
FIGURE 37 –MS SQL SERVER FORM 98
FIGURE 38 –MS EXCHANGE SERVER FORM 102
FIGURE 39 –EMAIL COMPONENTS FORM 103
FIGURE 40 –BACKUP SOLUTION FORM 106

Acknowledgements

This book would never have been created if it had not been for the countless engineers that I have encountered and worked with over the years. I must acknowledge all the engineers that have spent many a late night over cold pizza troubleshooting a network that had poor or incomplete documentation.

That 'just figure it out' pain and suffering we all went through was one of the biggest motivations I had that really drove my desire to get this book finished. Through the years, I have developed and implemented many process and procedures that are designed with a purpose in mind. That purpose being to save time and effort and to increase the value of the end results. Automation of repetitive tasks is often the first thing that comes to mind.

I would like to thank everybody for all those late night discussions through the years which would be virtually impossible to list them all. There are also a few individuals that I would like to mention by name because of their impact on me personally and to the industry as a whole.

I would like to first thank my wife Janet and my children; Heather, James, and Bradley, for all their patience and understanding as I wrote this book. Without whom, no amount of business success would ever be worth it. In addition, I would like to also thank Stephen Nickolyn for his support and ability to always put me 'back on track' all those years ago. I would like to thank T. Sean Teague, my business partner, and one of the greats in understanding our industry and how our work impacts the clients beyond the technical aspects. As well as their ability to listen to me complain and vent and providing that sage counsel to keep me on track.

In analyzing hundreds of consulting and support engineers and the way that they work, I have found that many of them have been frustrated with the lack of documentation that a client has about their network. I have coached and trained many engineers in how to develop usable network documentation that is also a quality deliverable. Within our own organization, we utilize the very same core process to quickly and effectively capture a client's network information in our documentation.

Through the years, I have incorporated the feedback from the professionals I have worked with to update the process and layout of the data that we collect. I hope that you find this book as helpful to you and your business, as we have found it for ours.

Introduction

Do I Need This Book?

If you are reading this section to determine if this book is right for you then the answer is a resounding yes! The fact that you are reading this paragraph means that you are looking to either document your network, or make your network documentation better. The methodology contained in this book will assist even the most seasoned network engineer. So whether you are a novice network administrator or senior networking consultant you will find the information contained here valuable.

Either way, this book will be a great asset to help you accomplish your goal, whether you are a network engineer, consultant or a business owner who relies upon the network. The systematic approach you will learn here will enable you to more easily create great looking, usable network support documentation that will be easy to maintain as well as be available when needed most.

Proper documentation is indispensable for the ongoing support of your network and proof of the work that has been done to the network. This book is intended to help network administrators, engineers and technicians document a computer network in an easy to accomplish and effective manner. While this book covers documenting a Windows Server-based network and associated infrastructure, the majority of this will carry over to a Linux, NetWare and/or Macintosh computing environments.

People are often tempted to say that they do not need a workbook or a structured method to document their network. I hear these types of objections all the time, especially from network engineers. The sad truth is that after many years working with businesses and IT consultants, I have noticed that more often than not they don't have a standard in place to document what they have. Frequently the "IT Guy" knows the network inside and out, but has all this "information" in his head and not consolidated to paper or even stored electronically off network. This information is critical to supporting your network and if you do not have proper documentation standards in place, you may be putting your business or your client's business at risk.

I have reviewed a wide variety of network documentation through the years, some good, some not so good. I have seen network documentation that was written on the back of paper napkins. As well, I've seen some pretty hefty documentation consisting of thousands of pages for a network with only twenty workstations and five servers. There is a lot of information that can be captured in documentation but if the important information is not captured and kept up to date then it did absolutely no good to collect it. If it is not kept current, then it is almost as bad as not having any at all.

Imagine this: It is 2am in the morning and your main domain controller has "crashed" or "hung up". You did your duty and created some documentation, but only had it stored on this server electronically. What do you do now? Did you have a "hard" copy or printed copy stored offsite or even onsite? What is your recovery process to bring this downed server back up? This book is designed to help you capture the information that you need to perform daily management, change management and troubleshooting, as well as to be a starting point for your disaster recovery plan. Disaster Recovery (DR) is a lengthy process and has many levels. There is not enough space in this book to dive deep into this subject although you will find references to your DR strategy and how the documentation that you will create with our process will help as a precursor to, and component of, your IT support and leadership strategy.

This book will walk you through capturing the key elements of your network in an easy, step-by-step manner. This will allow you to easily keep your documentation up to date as well as to have a reference document. This will save you time and money in support costs when you can pick up your documentation and quickly obtain the answer on a device configuration or the telephone number to your Internet Service Provider (ISP) when your internet connection stops working.

Can you retrieve a copy of your network documentation from a locker or your off-site storage location where it is sitting next to your Disaster Recovery (DR) backup tapes? Do you know with confidence that it is complete and updated? Are you confident that you could hand it to any network IT resource to troubleshoot an issue? If so, then congratulations!

Do you know beyond a shadow of a doubt, based solely on your current network documentation, you could hand it to a different network engineer to rebuild your network from the ground up? Then congratulations to you for having the foresight to clearly document your network. You are already on the right path and this book will help you add to your documentation or make parts of it easier to manage.

You might be tempted to say "I don't need a book to tell me how to document my network. I can sit down and write out the passwords and print configuration pages. I can build my own database or spreadsheet with this information." You could do this, and you might have already done so after reading the first few pages, but is that enough? Did you document everything? Can other people look at what you have collected and really know how the network is put together? Do you have the time to start from scratch, guessing at what should be documented, to accomplish this goal?

People tell me all the time they have documented their network then show me a spreadsheet with some passwords and maybe even some license keys for software. Sometimes they will actually have useful, up to date; information in a readable format but that is a rare occurrence. More often than not, they will have a spreadsheet with a lot of raw data where only they know how to read and extrapolate out needed answers. Or there might be a binder or a notebook with random pages sticking out and not very organized.

To be successful, you should have clear, concise, documentation of the network that is understandable to any IT person who may have to troubleshoot it. If it is only good for one person, then it is the equivalent to not having any documentation. What if that one person won the lottery? (I'll use the lottery analogy instead of the proverbial "hit by a bus" scenario....... let's think positive).

Short and sweet, you need this book if your network is not documented and kept up to date. If it is documented, then you will find some golden nuggets to enhance what you already have.

As an IT outsourcing company we have seen many situations that I find appalling. The top two are fairly universal and usually combined with other issues as well.

- Network backups - Either there are no backups of critical data or there are bad backups and no one was aware of the backup issue. Neither scenario is good. As an example, I worked with one company where backups were successful every day and they even had offsite backups that worked flawlessly. Their accounting system vendor had made updates and created a new database, migrated the existing data to the new database, but did not let the client know about the changes to the database files. Their large 250GB database had shrunk to less than 10mb. Their backup job ran successful but it was not backing up their core financial data. Had they had an outage or had to roll back to an earlier copy of the new database, they might have been out of business. In this case, we performed an audit of their data and compared it to what was being backed up and uncovered this issue.

- In my second example, the "IT Guy" has all the knowledge of the network in his head and he wins the lottery and left the business. (See, I am taking the positive approach). Frequently, when we take over supporting a network or perform an audit of a network, we spend a lot of time tracking down the previous administrators or even the former IT companies to obtain critical information that our client should already have known or have had documented.

If you've been in IT for long or have worked as a consultant, you are probably chuckling with a memory of the past and a knowing smile saying to yourself, "Yep, been there... done that." Think for a second, have you ever had to spend time tracking down information to resolve an issue when that information should have been previously documented?

How Its Organized

This book is designed and has been laid out for three target audiences. First, in no particular order, Network Administrators who do not want to lose their job or be thought of negatively for not documenting the network properly. Second, Network Consultants who support multiple client networks and want to rapidly find the information that they need and to show additional value to their existing and potential clients. Lastly, for the owners of small to medium sized business (SMB) and the IT Staff that support the network, the lifeblood of the business.

I've included sample forms and layouts that can be easily customized and tailored to your network. As we progress, I will explain in detail the importance of each section and how to capture the information we need for each form. In addition, you will understand why certain key aspects of the network are documented and the business functions that the technology supports. I've also included many standard scripts that I have developed over the years that help to capture the data in a format for easy transposing to the document forms. Many of these scripts will present the results, formatted in a printable or savable format, for the documentation, so that it can be incorporated more easily into the electronic documentation templates.

This workbook will become the "bible" or the definitive guide to supporting your business network. If there is a question about the network, the answer should be found in the bible.

The Hidden Value

Whether you are a business owner, responsible for a business network or an individual that has, supports, or just plain needs to audit a network--then this book is written for you. With the reliance upon technology today, more and more businesses are coming to the realization that their network is critical to their business. Many businesses lose thousands of dollars per hour if their network is broke. This is commonly referred to as "the network is down".

In the '90s many businesses were just beginning to implement or install their first network. With the new network they no longer were required to copy data to floppy disks and then walk the disk over to another computer in order to share data or files. Today, they save the data to a folder or network share on a server across the network from their workstation.

Today, businesses typically have at least one server, use email, access the internet and store key company data electronically. Many have a web site and use accounting software such as QuickBooks, Great Plains, Macola, and many other enterprise solutions. For the workstations, many use Microsoft Office or Open Office for productivity software in order to create and manipulate files such as spreadsheets, written documents, compose an email, etc. Although small to medium sized businesses may have less employees than a fortune 500 or 1000 company the network that drives their business can be just as critical and complex.

Stop and think for a minute how much you use a computer every day. Think about how often you share data via electronic communication, the email you just read or forgot to send out. What about the updates to that corporate spreadsheet showing the sales numbers for last month or the inventory of stock on hand. Did you develop a PowerPoint presentation last month? Are you able to read your email on your mobile phone? How did it get there?

Think about all those different types of documents that you have used over the past week. Where do you store them? Where did you find them? Where do your clients or employee's find them?

Now think about what happens when those documents or systems are not available when you need them. How do you get your email when the internet connection or your email servers are not working?

It's scary to think how much we use technology every day without a second thought to what it takes to keep it running. As a business owner, consultant, or IT person, you have probably experienced a time when the network was broken. As a business owner, this period of time, even a brief period of time, is very costly, and most do not realize just how much this costs the business.

Network downtime is when one or more elements of your network are not functioning properly. This may have an impact that is considered minor such as an issue that affects only one user. Major outages are issues where a key technology is not functioning or an issue that affects multiple users.

This is where good network documentation is invaluable. When troubleshooting an issue, proper documentation can sometimes mean the difference between minutes and days on the time it takes to repair the issue. Each and every one of those minutes can cost the business money and loss of goodwill. Good documentation and proper maintenance will help keep your costs down and productivity up.

Throughout this book, I will show you how to document a network in an organized and easily readable format.

Chapter 1 - Getting Prepared

Through the years I have worked with a wide variety of network documentation. Some have been great, in my opinion, and others I have found were not practical to use for supporting a network. I like to take the approach that it is better to have high quality, readily available information at your fingertips than to have a great looking document where it is difficult to find what you need. It is easy to capture lots and lots of data, make it look pretty and have a 900 page technical document, all accurate with lots of details. When you are done, there will probably only be about 40 to 100 pages of useful, day-to-day information. You can even present it to your boss, company executive, or client and give that "Wow" factor, thereby justifying all the time that you spent creating it.

This book is designed to help you get that 100 pages of useful information captured and documented in a reasonable format to make it easy to use as a reference book. Essentially, we will build a network in a book without having to start with collecting 900 pages of raw data. It's easy and you will find that it will become one of your most used tools. The network book that you create will also have that 'wow' factor besides being useful.

I have organized the documentation templates in a manner where you can use all or some of the template pages. We will cover them all, but each network is different and will have minor differences that make the environment unique. As we progress, you will find that you may want to add more sections or additional data. I have created a notes section and an appendix for miscellaneous information to make this easy for you. Often overlooked or viewed with dread, documenting is easy with a little leadership.

Things you need to document a network.

- Pen
- Paper (use a yellow 8x11pad)
- 3 ring binder
- 2 packs of 3-hole dividers (I prefer 5 tab, but many people use 8 tab)
- And a network of course... (have to have one in order to document it)

Recommended:

- A computer with Microsoft Office installed with the following applications:
- Word
- Excel
- Access
- Visio

These will allow you to create, modify, and edit the documentation like a professional. In addition, they will let you make changes and reprint all or part of the documentation with ease. I recommend using a three ring binder that has the clear sleeves on the outside and pouches on the inside. Typically a 1" binder is where I start. If I have more than 50 workstations and servers then I would recommend starting with a slightly larger binder or possibly divide the documentation into two parts, core network and workstation information. During a network down emergency, the core network and server information is typically the information that is needed most.

With pen and paper in hand, make a quick list of what equipment that you have and collect what documentation that you may have already. If you have been diligent, you may even have a three ring binder of what the network was like two years ago, with lots of loose pages tucked in there of extra information or you may have nothing at all, a clean slate as a starting point. Either way, you will create a brand new, up to date, document reflecting your current state of the network. The new network documentation book will be able to be relied upon, easily updated and expanded for daily support needs as well as disaster recovery purposes.

> *Note: You can cheat and use Excel to create the inventory list of equipment instead of using just pen and paper. Remember, though, that you will still need pen and paper as we go along.*
>
> *Author TIP: I usually print out a blank copy of the template, and use a combination of the electronic copy and the blank hard copy for manually collection of data as needed, and then transfer to the electronic version.*

I begin by creating a title page and cover for the binder. I keep it simple by putting the company name, a title for the document, date created, date edited, and who created it. Usually the title is very simple like "Network Documentation". I use a bold font for the company name and title, typically 24 or 28 point font. I print two copies, one goes in the outer sleeve of the binder, and one is 3-hole punched and is the first page in the binder. In addition, I go ahead place the dividers into the binder behind this title page.

If you are following my lead on this, we now have a network documentation book. Congratulations, you have taken the first step of a successful journey. We will use this constantly as we progress to fill it with all the useful information about your network. I work from start to finish through the documentation process. After this chapter, you may choose to skip around and complete the sections in a different order. If this is your first documentation book using this process I recommend that you follow my lead, step by step to maximize the results of your first book project. Remember the checklist and keep it updated as we progress throughout this project.

Your next step will be to identify what needs to be audited. We will start with a simple network diagram and the initial inventory list.

Don't worry if you miss some items on the first pass. Usually, you will find that as you audit, you will uncover devices that you did not remember on the first round. This is normal, so do not panic or fret. Let's have fun and enjoy ourselves as we do this together.

Basic Network Diagram

Here is where we draw a basic schematic or diagram of your network. This is a big picture view of how your network works and is connected. First, take a piece of paper (from your scratch pad) and draw a basic overview of how everything logically fits together. See the example below of a simple network diagram.

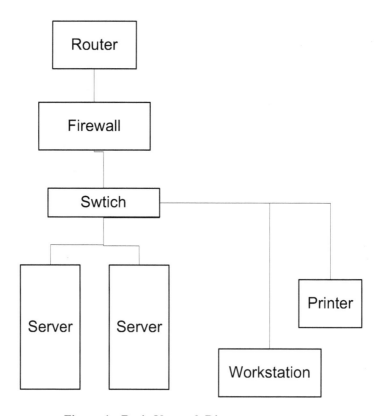

Figure 1 - Basic Network Diagram

Draw the appropriate number of devices for each category. We will do a more detailed diagram toward the end of this book. The final diagram will include a lot of the key information that we collect along the way. This is just for you to have an understanding of what you have and how it works. There are many ways to draw a network, and we will use several of them over the course of this book. Over time you will get a feel for when to use each type. In this case, you just need to jot down a simple overview that can be used to get an outline of the network that we are going to audit.

Take a moment to review your network. You may be lucky enough to already have a picture in your mind. If so, that means you know a good deal already about your network, and that will boost your confidence as we get that information down on paper. Let me take a moment to discuss the diagram above and the basic function that each component serves in your network.

The components listed in the figure 1:

- **Router** – A router is a device or appliance that connects your network to the outside world, and possibly one or more remote office locations as well. In some cases, you may have a router separating two or more sections of your network within the same office.

- **Firewall** – A firewall is a device or appliance that helps to protect your network and acts as a barrier between the Internet and your local network. Sometimes your router may also serve as the firewall if it has that capability built in.

- **Switch** – A switch is where network cables centrally terminate so that your network devices can talk to each other. You may have more than one switch in your environment. You may also have additional switches around the office that split one network connection into many others.

- **Server** – This is the computer or computers that are typically running Microsoft (MS) Windows Server, Linux or Novell

NetWare operating systems. They may perform many functions in your environment. Most commonly these functions include file storage, print, email, database, and client/server applications to users of the network. A network may have only one server, or it might have 500. Regardless of the number of servers you have, this process can be used to successfully document your network.

- **Workstation** – These may be desktop computers or notebook computers. If you are running Microsoft Terminal Services and/or Citrix servers then you may also have Thin Client devices. These are devices that run remote sessions from the server. If you do not know whether or not you have them, then most likely you do not. We will know for sure when we are through auditing your network.

- **Printer** – For our purposes we will work with networked printers. This means printers that are attached and accessible via the network. Usually means that you have setup a print driver/queue on the server, and then configure the workstations to connect to the printer via the share name on the server. Typically this means that a network cable is plugged in to the printer or a print device attached to the printer.

There probably will be many other types of devices on your network, and we will get to those. You might even add them to the diagram as you identify them. Our first pass is to get the basics down on paper as a starting point. I am sure as we go, there will be additional items to add to the list. Like that laser printer in the accounting department or the big office copier/printer that the marketing department uses for high volume printing.

As you draw out your, simple, network diagram, add the device names for each. This will allow you to more easily transfer this information to the inventory list.

Inventory list

The inventory list will be the starting point of the audit. This will be a checklist of what will be documented. It is okay for the list to be incomplete at this stage. This is just the starting point and it will be added to it as we progress through the auditing. The following list can be created in Excel to make it easy to read when you print it. This will make it easy to make edits, additions, and changes too.

Device Name	Type	Function	Location

Figure 2 - Inventory List Template

Description of what information to collect:

- **Device Name** – Usually the actual computer/device name. Some devices such as routers, printers, etc. may not have a true device name itself, for those devices, use the network reference name, or create a unique name to reference it. This will make it easier to track and identify.

- **Type** – This is a general high level description of the type of device, i.e. server, printer, router, firewall, switch, etc. This will help you to organize the devices by logical grouping as you audit the network.

- **Function** –The description of what the device does or provides to your network. A server may provide file and print services, or it might provide email or database servers to name a few examples.

- **Location** – A short description of where the device is physically located. This could be listed as server room, rack2 or accounting department or any other reference that is easy to identify. You might give references by landmark. An example might be: Under the desk in accounting by Susie's desk. That will be okay for now. We will build more specific, location references as we go. In this example, what happens to the reference if Susie moves to a different part of the office or leaves the company. What if you win the lottery and the new IT guy can't find Susie's desk? He/she may not even know Susie. This is why it is important to be clear in your documentation and to keep it current.

Device Name	Type	Function	Location
FP001	Server	File, Print	Server Rack 1
Dalrtr-1	Router	Internet router	Telco closet
Sw16-2	Switch	Eth. Switch	Closet, 16th floor

Figure 3 - Inventory List Example

Author TIP: When working through a section that I do not have complete information. I format the missing data areas in red text with a yellow background. This makes it easy for me to rapidly identify uncollected or incomplete data.

If you are not using MS Word or Excel then I would recommend getting the red page arrow stickers that you can apply pointing to the sections on the page where you may need to input or complete the missing information.

Personally, I like to use a little bit more of an advanced list format. This format lets you input the devices under each category and will give you a quick snapshot of what, and how many, devices that need to be audited.

Device Name	Type	Function	Location
Servers			
Routers, Firewalls			
Switches			
Network Printers and Scanners			

Figure 4 - Advanced Inventory list template

In addition, this also helps you to later expand the template with the appropriate number of device worksheets in advance of performing the actual auditing and data collection steps. As we work through the document, we will fill in the gaps. Sometimes as you work through a section, you will not have all the necessary data to complete the template. This is okay. We will put in a place marker to make it easy to see what areas have not been completed.

27

Chapter 2 – Basic Information

Contact List

General Contacts

The first section of the network documentation book we will work on is your contact list. The list is divided into several groups to make it easy to find who you need to reach. There are several groups of contacts that you capture. This will need to be updated periodically. It is not fun to try and reach someone at 2 AM in the morning, especially if you have to spend time tracking down the right phone number to reach them.

We will develop several different contact lists for this section. The first list is for your internal organizational or company contacts that are either technical or key personnel. This is normally ranked by whom to call, in the order of priority, during a network emergency or network issue. This list may be used by non-IT staff and IT staff alike to obtain assistance or to notify IT staff to report a network outage or issue. This list will normally include all IT related staff members as well as key executives. Other people in the company may be included as well, such as department managers. You may even segment the list to separate the IT/Key personnel from the department managers. Either way, it should clearly show, top to bottom, the order in which make calls in case of an emergency.

Contact	Office	Home	Mobile	Email
*Joe Blow	123.456.7890	123.456.7890	123.456.7890	jblow@xyz.com
Suzy Q	123.456.7890	123.456.7890	123.456.7890	jblow@xyz.com
* Primary Technical Contacts				

Figure 5- Internal Contacts

Escalation Contacts

This list is for technical support contacts, people to call in order of priority, or escalation for specific technical issues. You might subcategorize this list by type of technical issue if your support is structured in such a way where you split out different technical responsibilities, such as server support and desktop support. There are many ways to group based upon how your business is organized. (See figure 6 where an example is separated out by support category for desktop and server).

You might choose to split or break out this list by more specific technologies or job roles, such as email support, database, custom application support. Take a minute to think about which person handle's what type of issues in your organization and then you can more realistically complete this section. It is okay to have only one person on the entire list, or 50, depending on the size of the organization and the support requirements.

Contact	Office	Home	Mobile	Email
Desktop Support				
*Joe Blow	123.456.7890	123.456.7890	123.456.7890	jblow@xyz.com
Suzy Q	123.456.7890	123.456.7890	123.456.7890	jblow@xyz.com
Server Support				
*John Doe	123.456.7890	123.456.7890	123.456.7890	jdoe@xyz.com
Mary ABC	123.456.7890	123.456.7890	123.456.7890	jdoe@xyz.com
* Primary Technical Contacts				

Figure 6 - Escalation List

Vendor Support

The vendor support list is more than just how to contact the vendor. You may need to capture more information for some vendors. Typically each vendor requires additional information in order to provide support. Information such as contract numbers or warranty information may need to be captured here. The goal is to have the information the vendor requires from you when you call in for support so that you do not have to search for it.

This list will usually include hardware and software support contacts to call when support is required or needs to be escalated beyond your internal staff. I recommend the list be sorted alphabetically by the vendor name. Depending upon the number of technologies in your environment, this list might be long. In that instance, you might group your contacts by broad categories such as software, hardware, etc.

Company	Contact	Office	Mobile	Email
Compaq	Greg H.	123.456.7890	123.456.7890	jblow@xyz.com
Contract Number: Notes:				
Dell	Jimmy J.	123.456.7890	123.456.7890	jblow@xyz.com
Contract Number: Notes:				

Figure 7 - Vendor Tech Support

Telco/ISP Contacts

This list is for telecom and internet service providers. This will usually include notes of specific Circuit IDs or IP addresses of routers to help escalation for specific technical issues. If you have multiple carriers or locations, you might subcategorize this list by location or regions.

Company	Contact	Office	Mobile	Email
Telco Co.	Jim K.	123.456.7890	123.456.7890	jblow@xyz.com
Contract Number: Notes:		Circuit ID:		
ISP Co.	Jimmy J.	123.456.7890	123.456.7890	jblow@xyz.com
Contract Number: Notes:		IP Address:		

Figure 8 - Telco Contact List

Site Location Information

This is where you will document the address and who the main contact is for each location that is to be supported or has connections to the network in some way. It is good to also document information such as the location of where key devices are located, how to get to the servers, and other notes of interest. This is a good place for summarizing where key devices are located so that when you call the site's primary contact (smart hands on site), you can direct them rapidly to where the effected device is located. This is also a good spot to have the refresher so that you (who might be calling the site) do not have to flip through the book to find the information. The purpose of the book is to have information readily available at your fingertips. There will be some duplication of information where it makes sense. It is important to keep all the information as updated as possible.

The Site Name is used as a common reference to the location. Typically, this reflects how the business commonly references or has named the location. You will want to include the physical address and main phone numbers to this site. In addition, it is best practice to include the contact information for the primary or smart hands person. Remember to include all the contact phone numbers for this person, as you may need to reach them after business hours.

It is recommended that you include notes for each site, such as driving directions, what entrance to use, where key devices are located. You should have one section completed for each site.

The example below shows a completed site form for two locations. Notice that the notes section has custom driving directions as well as location to the core network devices.

Site Name:	Dallas Corporate		Y	Primary Site

Address:		**Primary Contact:**	
	12345 Somewhere Ave	**Name:**	John Doe
	Building K	**Direct Phone:**	(555) 123-4567
	Nowhere, IN 111111	**Home:**	(555) 123-4567
Office Phone:	(555) 123-4567	**Mobile:**	(555) 123-4567
Office Fax:	(555) 123-4567	**Email:**	Jdoe@jxyz.com

Notes: Turn left off of highway, parking in attached building
Use South Entrance.
Server room is located on 14th floor and has all core Network Infrastructure and Telco Dmarc.
15th floor has switch closet that feeds floors 15, 16 and 17 with a homerun to the server room.

Site Name:	Tyler Production		N	Primary Site

Address:		**Primary Contact:**	
	12345 Nowhere Street	Name:	Jim Jones
	Suite b	Direct Phone:	(555) 123-4567
	Tyler, TX 111111	Home:	(555) 123-4567
Office Phone:	(555) 123-4567	Mobile:	(555) 123-4567
Office Fax:	(555) 123-4567	Email:	jjones@tyler.xyz.com

Notes:
Server room has all network equipment.

Figure 9 – Site Location Information

Network Overview

The Network Overview consists of two main sections, the Network Summary and the Network Diagram. These two sections may be included on a single page depending on the complexity of the network and how detailed you choose to go at this point in the documentation. Typically, I try to have this take no more than two pages total if we are not able to get a comfortable summary level on one page. The network overview is the really high level description of the network with a simple network diagram to represent key aspects of the environment.

The network summary is usually one to two paragraphs describing the network in plain English. This is the non-technical description or executive overview of the network. It should include items such as the server operating system, email solution, server based applications and databases. Telco items should include what type of connectivity to the Internet is in use. Are there Virtual Private Network (VPN) connections between sites or for remote users? What type of firewall is in place? What kind of corporate virus protection or backup solution is in place today? In addition, we need to describe what software is on the desktops/laptops. What are the key applications installed from the company perspective that the users utilize. Take care to note the line of business (LOB) applications or applications that are custom or proprietary to the type of business or that is key to running the business.

The network diagram is usually a half page diagram. I have standardized on Microsoft Visio software to develop the diagrams and schematics for my clients. Feel free to use whatever application that you are comfortable using or that you are already familiar with. I recommend that when inserting your diagrams into the document that you utilize MS Word's feature to Paste Special as a MS Picture or Enhanced Picture. This helps to reduce the size of the finished document, although it does not allow you to edit the diagram from within MS Word. In order to edit or make changes to the diagram you will have to go back to the original drawing and then edit and replace the diagram back into the network documentation.

> **TIP:**
>
> - *To keep the size of the document from growing astronomically, paste the pictures and diagrams as MS (Enhanced) Picture.*
> - *I recommend that you create a one by one (1x1) cell table and then paste your picture within this cell. This will help to keep your picture size on the page where you want it. If not, you may have to resize it manually on the page.*
> - *If you have a more complex network, your network diagram may need to go on a separate page. In this case, I recommend that you paste the diagram in landscape mode to increase the readability of the diagram. In this scenario, the top of the diagram should be on the left side of the page, and the left side of the diagram should be on the bottom of the page.*

Network Overview Example

ABC Company utilizes Microsoft Windows Server 2003 as its primary Network Operating System (NOS). In addition, ABC Company utilizes Microsoft Windows Terminal Services to provide for remote network access. Currently it is utilizing Microsoft Exchange Server 2003 as its corporate email solution.

ABC Company uses Symantec Backup Exec v10d backup software, which is installed on the <<serverName>> server with the MS Exchange and remote server backup agent. In addition, the Advanced Open File Option (AOFO) is installed and configured for <serverName> server.

ABC Company utilizes _____ for virus protection at the server and desktop level. The central management console is installed on <<serverName>> server.

The Local Area Network (LAN) Infrastructure consists of a two Ethernet switches. The Ethernet switch and hubs provides connectivity for the network servers as well as the Internet firewall. The Ethernet switch and hubs provides connectivity for workstations and printers that attach at 10/100mb. Primary Internet access is provided via the____line circuit to its Internet Service Provider (ISP).

All workstations are running _<VISTA, WinXP Pro>_ as the primary desktop operating systems (OS). End-users utilize _____ for its back office productivity applications and email client software.

Network Diagram

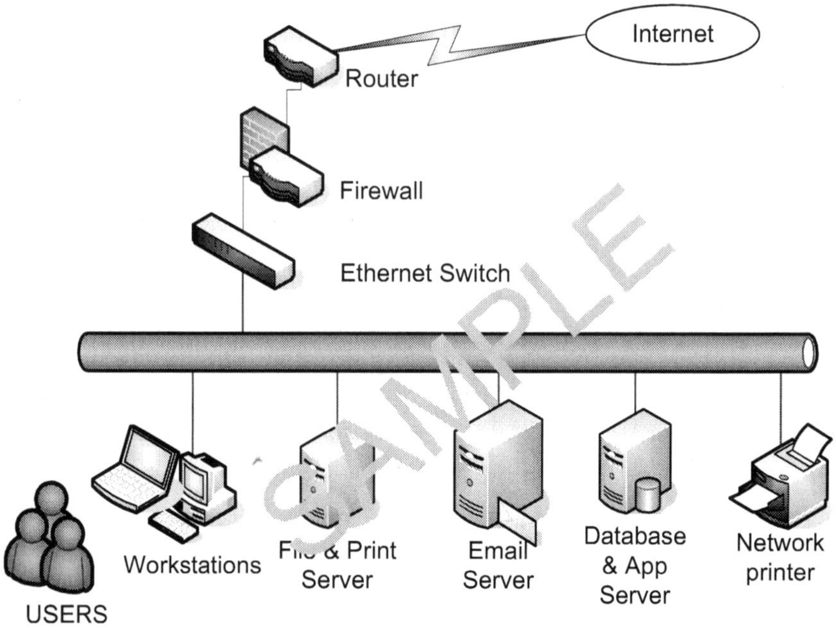

Figure 10 – Example Network Diagram

Network Environment

For each location with a network server, the network environment page should be included. The site name should be filled in at the top of each page. This identifies which site that the specific information covers. This is the information that helps to quickly identify where the key equipment is physically located and the environment in which they reside. This data should be reviewed periodically for accuracy, as well as for changes that may need to be made. For example, if you replace a server every year due to moisture damage and the server is in a room that does not have a dehumidifier then it would be good to identify this earlier, rather than later. Often we find that by taking the time to document the environment separately from the rest of the documentation, we are able to analyze this by itself. After you complete this for all your sites, review it, and see if there are changes that need to be made to perhaps pre-empt or head off an issue before it occurs.

Building Location of Key Equipment - You should enter a short descriptive paragraph on where the key network equipment is located in your office or building. This should include the servers, routers, and firewalls primarily.

Location of Servers – Describe the physical installation of the servers. Are they in a rack, on the floor or on a table in the conference room? Be sure to describe how to get there when you enter the office. Describe this as you would to somebody who was unfamiliar with your office layout.

Security of the Server – This section is important, as we are now discussing network security. Network security is not just how do people log in and access the Internet. Physical security is one of the most often overlooked aspects of network management. You should look at how easy is it to get to the servers. Are they locked in a secure room, or can somebody walk in and easily pick them up and carry them out.

Lighting – Simply put, this is whether the equipment room is well lit or not. Is it dark and hard to see, or is there enough light to see behind the equipment.

Condition of Cable – Here we are going to describe the network cabling and organization. What type of cabling is being used? Is it in good condition? Are the cables the appropriate length? Are there any nicks or cuts in the cables. Is there any cable management in place? These are questions that will help complete this section.

Notes – This is where you will write down your personal observations of what you see. Look at the environment, is it the server room, or Telco closet. Write down what you see, as it is. It is okay to be critical. This is not a time to be complimentary, but rather look for the flaws and trouble spots. We are documenting what is, not what it should be like. We will use this information to help develop the plan and tasks to get us where we want to be if we are not already there.

Network Environment Example

Site Name: _____

Building Location of Key Equipment:

All servers and network equipment are located in a dedicated server room on the same floor as the corporate offices. Network battery backups are located in dedicated storage areas on the same floor, but not in same room as the servers.

Location of Servers:

The servers are located in an open rack that is shared with other network equipment. The rack contains the monitor, keyboard and KVM for all servers. Entry to the server room is located across the hall from the receptionist desk.

Security of the Server:

The servers and network equipment are in an unlocked room.

Lighting:

The lighting is adequate for all necessary operations that would occur in the server room.

Condition of Cable:

The cabling appears to be of high quality with no visible defects. There is no cable management installed on the racks. Patch cables are not neatly organized.

Notes:

Lack of cable management makes it difficult to troubleshoot connections.

Be cautious on lower switches, cables do not seat well.

Chapter 3 – Internet & Telco

Internet Domain Registration Information

This section covers your internet domain name registration and corresponding public DNS servers. The Internet domain name is a unique naming convention. This naming convention prevents duplicate names being present on the Internet. The internet domain name is mapped to a public IP address. Similar to how your house is associated with its street address in a public address or phone book. The public domain name and the address information are typically stored on somebody else's network. The public domain name and its information are what other people use to find things like your website, look up the address of your mail server to send email to someone and a host of other reasons.

However, it is NOT like a yellow page's ad, where it is optional to post your information. If you have a registered internet domain name, then you have to keep it registered in order to continue using it. If you have any services available on the internet, such as a website or email, then you would use the domain name instead of its IP address.

This information is important to keep handy. You do not want to let a domain name lapse that you use. It is important to handle domain renewals prior to their expiration. As domain names are unique, if you let the domain registration expire, somebody else might register your domain name. This can be disastrous for your business. Your customers might one day, all of a sudden, start arriving at a competitor's web site or your email might just stop working.

It is important to keep this information updated and available. If you have to troubleshoot a DNS issue, or make changes to your records, you will need to have this information readily available.

The form is kept simple and basic. There is no need to make it complex. We begin by identifying what Domain name we are documenting and who owns the domain. We'll make a note of the expiration for each domain. This is an important date to know so you can ensure notifying the right person to handle the renewal in advance or for you to handle the renewal before it expires.

You need to know the registrar name and contact information. The registrar is the company with whom the domain is registered. You also need to know whom the administrative, technical, and billing contact for each domain that is registered. The contacts may all be the same person, or it may be different people within your organization. In some instances, you may have a 3rd party person listed under the technical contact. It is best practice to register each domain name under the business name as the owner. If the name is registered under an individual then that individual owns the name and not the business. If that individual leaves the business on non-favorable terms then they may be inclined to not assist in transferring ownership back to the business.

We also need to document the public DNS settings for the first and second DNS Servers that host the Domain address information. If you use a public registrar that also hosts your public DNS records, then you will need to be able to login and have access to be able to change those settings when necessary.

If your DNS address records are hosted separately from your DNS registrar, be sure to document it in the notes section. This will provide adequate information in the event that changes are required, or assist in troubleshooting issues. You will need to copy both pages for each domain that you have registered. You may need to copy the DNS host record sheet more than once depending on the number of 'hosts' or names that you have. I recommend that you document all of your IP addresses to host records, so that in the event that you change ISP's, you can easily see what records need to be changed, added or edited. This is frequently called the zone information. There will be two sources for each public DNS zone. The first is the primary or master which is where changes are made. Next is the secondary which holds a downstream copy of the master zone information. This provides redundancy in case the primary server is not available so that users will still be able obtain the address of where to go.

This form is for your Public or Internet Domain Information (Public DNS zones) and not for your internal Windows Domain. If you host a copy of your DNS inside your network, you will need to complete a DNS host record sheet for it as well. We will cover your Windows domain information elsewhere in our documentation.

Note: *Remember to complete Public DNS host record sheets for your internal DNS zones if you host DNS records on your internal servers that use different IP addresses than external users.*

For example: access to a corporate website; www.corpname.com.

Outside your network, such as at a customer site, this would resolve to the public IP address of the website and the customer would then connect to the website across the Internet.

For your users inside your network, they would need the IP address to be the internal address of the local server. Your corporate employee's will not go to the internet and back inside the network and connect. Most firewalls do not allow traffic to loop around, or make that kind of U-Turn and come back inside the network.

Domain Registration Information

Company/Organization: _____

Domain Name: _____

Last Updated: __ / __ / __
Registration Expires: __ / __ / __

Registrar:

Phone: _____

MGMT URL: Http:// _____

Admin Account: _____

Password: _____

Administrative Contact:

Email: _____

NIC Handle/User _____

Phone: _____

Technical Contact

Email: _____

NIC Handle/User _____

Phone: _____

Billing Contact

Email: _____

NIC Handle/User _____

Phone: _____

Primary DNS

Server Name: _____

IP Address _____

Secondary DNS

Server Name: _____

IP Address _____

Notes:

Figure 11 – Domain Name Registration Form

Public DNS Host Record Sheet

Domain Name:

_____

Host/Node	Type (A, CName, MX)	IP address (Public)
Example: Mail.<YourDomainNAme.com>	*MX 10*	*Aaa.bbb.ccc.ddd*

Figure 12 – Public DNS Host Form

Internet Service Provider Information

In this section we will capture the pertinent information relating to your Internet Service Provider. Many times this is will be separate from the Telco provider, but more often than not, it is the same provider. Although the Internet services are typically handled separately, knowing who to call during an issue is crucial.

I separate the ISP from the Telco information to minimize redundant information as well as to consolidate other key data. If you have a single network with only one site, this could be as straight forward as completing one set of information. If you have multiple locations, then you will appreciate the ease of finding the right information faster. Having multiple sites with one carrier for Internet services gives you one provider to deal with, making troubleshooting easier. As you can guess, however, this is not the typical IT environment.

All too often, when an outage occurs, we hear how support people are scrambling to figure out which provider covers the affected site. Support staff must then run around to get the right contacts and contract information to be able to escalate a ticket with the correct ISP provider. This is an area of documentation that I have frequently found to be lacking or incomplete. A red flag, if you will.

Here we document all the key information such as provider name, contact numbers and email addresses. Many ISP providers monitor the statistics of your connection and provide a user interface that you may utilize to see these statistics and reports. In addition, we will write down the web URI login so you can access and see the traffic and uptime statistics, if available. Usually, there is also a web login for submitting requests for support. You will also want to document what equipment, if any, that the provider has installed onsite. This is typically called premise equipment because it is onsite at your location. It is important to know who owns the premise equipment.

Additionally you will document all the key IP address information that the provider has assigned. The Public IP address table allows us to put this information into the document for each site so that you know all the addresses that have been assigned.

Internet Service Provider Information

Provider:			
Contract/Account #:			
Web URL:			
Web/Traffic URL:			
Admin Username:			
Password:			

Company	Contact	Office	Email

Contract Number:
Notes:

Figure 13 – Example Internet Service Provider Form

Public IP Addresses

Site Name	IP Range	Def Gateway	Subnet	DNS1/DNS2

Figure 14 – Example ISP Site Address Information

Telco Provider Information

This form is similar to the ISP provider information that we discussed above. The primary difference is that this form is for the Telco carrier. The lower part of the form is where you will document the specifics of the Telco circuits and equipment for each provider. I usually group this by vendor and site location. Networks may have multiple locations where one Telco vendor provides services for both voice and data or multiple types of services for each category. As well, there may be more than one vendor for the voice and data services.

For example, you might have one vendor provide voice or telephone lines, another vendor providing Internet connectivity, and a third vendor providing point to point network connections between different locations. These types of scenarios are why you need to be diligent in capturing this information. When there are issues with the Telco services, you will need to be able to quickly identify which line it is, the associated equipment, and who to call.

TIP: *Keep the Public IP address table updated helps in troubleshooting to rapidly check a site's connectivity. By knowing the default gateway, you are able to quickly ping its IP address and, if you get a response, then we can move inward to the next device onsite.*

If you get no response, then the next step might be to check with the Telco provider for status on the circuit.

Telco Provider Information

Provider:	
Contract/Account #:	
Web URL:	
Web/Traffic URL:	
Admin Username:	
Password:	

Company	Contact	Office	Email

Contract Number:
Notes:

Figure 15 – Example Telco Provider Form

Circuit Information

Site Name	Type(DSL,T-1)	Circuit ID	Provider	Provisioned Equipment

Figure 16 – Example Telco Site Address Information

Router Configuration

The router configuration form is very similar to the firewall configuration form that we will cover. Most firewalls are very specialized routers even though they do not route traffic and many routers have firewall capabilities built in to them. Depending on your network and the router/firewall combination, you may only need to complete the firewall form. I would caution that as these are different forms, only the top part is basically the same, the remaining portions will still need to be completed for an accurate audit.

This information is pretty straight forward and should be easy to obtain. It is good to match this up to the Telco circuit ID for each router. This will help during troubleshooting if it is a Telco issue and not an actual router issue.

Like the firewall, you will want to backup the router's binary image and store it on the server and back it up. In addition, if your router can print out a configuration file in an easy to read format, like most Cisco products, then I highly recommend that you either print it out, or copy it into a text file to include within the documentation. Many devices have a graphical user interface, commonly referred to as a GUI. Devices that only use a GUI to manage and configure do not always have an export feature to capture the text or readable configuration. In these instances, you will want to go through each screen to capture the information as well as maybe do screenshots to a word file to print out later and put in the documentation book.

I use the notes section to record custom configurations, VPN information, and hard coded routes. A route is a path that a router knows to direct traffic to a remote destination. This will allow you to easily recreate the configuration in a disaster recovery scenario. Always keep track of the support contracts, like firewalls, most router manufactures have some form of renewable warranty or support contract. Most of these give you access to updates and technical support. If you let the support lapse, it can be quite frustrating trying to get help and support, or worse yet, be in a network down (outage) situation, and not have your hardware covered. Most vendors will have fee based support either by incident or hourly to help you in this situation. Typically the initial cost for one call is two to three times the cost of what the support contract would have been. Have you ever had to buy a new device because you could not get the support on the high dollar router you invested in due to letting the maintenance contract expire?

> *TIP:* *I recommend to always backup the router and firewall configurations to disk. I prefer to backup to a server, into an IT directory that is secured as well as backed up. In addition, I usually recommend archiving these files to a CD or DVD along with other specialty files, like device drivers, firmware patches, etc.*
>
> *If you have ever had to rebuild a router or firewall without Internet access to obtain software, drivers or patches, then you know what a headache it is not having this readily available.*

Router Configuration

Make and Model _____

Serial Number: _____

Warranty/Support Contract#: _____

Start Date: _____ **End Date:** _____ **Renewable?** _____

Firmware Version _____ **Revision:** _____

OS/IOS Version _____ **Revision:** _____

Support Contact: _____

Contract Information/Password: _____

Telco Circuit ID: _____

PPPOE User _____

Password: _____

LAN/Internal IP		WAN/External IP		Security/Device	
IP		IP		User Name:	
SN		SN			
GW		GW		Password:	
IP		IP			
DNS1		DNS1			
DNS2		DNS2			

Notes

Figure 17 – Router Configuration Form

54

Chapter 4 - Network Security

The security of the network is an important topic to discuss. I think that this topic is so hot that I'll say it again; network security is important. While there are many aspects and perspectives on how to secure a network, we are not going to go in depth and discuss security and strategies. This book is for documenting your network, not on how to manage or handle the security of the network. I could spend days on end just scratching the surface with you about network security. From a network security perspective, the first step is to audit and document what you have and how it is configured. With this in mind, the network bible we are developing will be your first step in determining whether your network is or is not reasonably secure.

Password Policy

For the initial documentation that we are creating, the first step is to document how the network security is configured in relation to the users' passwords and login times (when a user is allowed to access the network).

If you are managing the network, I recommend that you implement a basic password policy that, at a minimum, has the following characteristics:

- Minimum password length (number of characters that are required)
- Require at least one special character
- Change the passwords often
- Do not allow old passwords to be reused (keep at least a rolling count of three)

Password Security – To start, let's look at the Network or Domain security policy and complete the fields on the next page under password security. This tells us how the security policy is enforced or not enforced as the case may be.

Network Security – The next step will be to open up the administrative console applet for Users and Computers. We want to look at the Domain Administrators group and write down who and/or what groups are in this admin group. If there are sub groups in there, track them down to find who the actual members are of each group. In the documentation, we want to list both the users and the groups that are explicitly given administrative privileges. This is important to dig down to the individual users in each sub group as you might find that users in the organization have inherited rights or permissions that they should not have.

If there is a firewall in place, and there usually is of some type, document what kind it is. You will capture the specifics on how it is configured elsewhere in this book. Here we just want to know whether or not we have one and the make and model of it.

Server Room Security – This is where you document how physical access to the server room/data center is managed. This should be covered in good, descriptive detail.

Workstation Shares – Depending on the size of the environment, this may require scripting or other management tools to gather the security permissions if many workstations have shares. If you are able, at least examine a portion of workstations to see if there are shared resources and document the security for those resources; i.e. the everybody group has full control for file shares. This will at least give you a feel for how security is being managed at the workstation level. You can always come back to audit each one.

I recommend that if the results of the network security settings do not meet the requirements of the business then please discuss with the decision maker(s), or powers that be, on how the existing settings do not meet the criteria and discuss your security conscious recommendations.

I would recommend that you put together a simple policy document that you can present during the discussion that could also be used to send to the actual end-users in plain English. If you were to just go in and change the policy, push it out to the user community, and not explain the changes then you would get a lot of support calls for the proverbial "I can't login" or "it keeps telling me that it won't accept my password change". Neither of these two scenarios is helpful to your peace of mind.

Below is an example worksheet of a policy that you might look at utilizing in developing your network security policy.

Network Security Policy Worksheet

The following are the minimum items to review:

Password Length = _____ characters (should include numbers, letters, and at least one special character such as !@#$......

Maximum Password Age = _____ days (should be no more than 180 days, but 90 days is common. More frequently changing passwords will increase the support calls for forgotten passwords.

Password History Length = ___ (# recent passwords that cannot be re-used)

Lockout Threshold - ___ # of failed login attempts

Lockout Duration = ___ Minutes (how long to keep the account locked (recommended to have this at a minimum of 30 Minutes)

Lockout Observation Window = ___ minutes (time that the # of failed logins must occur before locking out the account

---

Group Policies

There are a multitude of items and settings that can be managed thru group policies in Active Directory. To begin with, in a Windows AD Network, Group Policies are part of the Domain administration abilities that allows you to implement specific configurations for users and computers. Group Policy settings are contained in Group Policy objects (GPOs). These are linked to the AD directory services containers for sites, domains, or organizational units (OUs).

The settings within each GPO are then applied to the selected target items using the hierarchical nature of Active Directory. This means that Group Policies are one of the top benefits in deploying Active Directory because it allows you to manage user and computer objects in keeping with the centralized management philosophy.

Group Policy Objects (GPO = policy) provides the ability in which to provide users with consistent access to their applications, application settings, additional security tweaks, roaming user profiles, and user data, from any managed computer—even when they are disconnected from the network.

Group Policies are configured through the use of two main tools:

Group Policy Object Editor, (previously known as the Group Policy snap-in, Group Policy Editor, or GPedit)

Group Policy Management Console (GPMC), available for download from the Microsoft Web site. Whereas Group Policy Object Editor is used to configure and modify settings within GPOs, GPMC is used to create, view, and manage GPOs

This book is for documenting a network, not teaching how/when/management of Group Policies. From the Group Policy Management Console, you can export html reports to help capture the current custom GPO settings that are implemented.

Network Security

Password Security

Length of Passwords:

Age of Passwords: _____

Computer Role   _____

Domain Name   _____

Primary Domain Controller   _____

Forced Logoff Time   _____

Min / Max Password Age   _____

Minimum Password Length   _____

Password History Length   _____

Lockout Threshold   _____

Lockout Duration   _____

Lockout Observation Window   _____
                                                     _____

Network Security

Number of persons with administrator rights:

Admin Users List: _____

                                                     _____

Is there a firewall in place? What type?

Server Room Security   _____

Workstation Shares

Figure 18 – Network Security Basic Form

59

Network Passwords

This template allows you to capture and record all your passwords in one location. While using this form you may want to change and possibly add additional fields depending on the login and password requirements.

As you document your network, you will no doubt find more areas that need further documentation. That is the flexibility of what we are doing. You can always add more. I have yet to find a network that was so well documented, that you could not find gaps or areas in the documentation. This is normal, so do not fret, after you have completed the core documentation you will want to review it, and as you do, you will find more to go back and document.

Documenting network passwords is something to be careful of. It is good to keep archived copies of the passwords in a secure location. We find it useful, and have had to refer back to the archives on a few occasions. Like when an application has a data restore performed, and the application has the password security stored in the files that were erased. This can be frustrating if you do not have adequate documentation including what the old password is.

I remember one instance where a client had a database application that he restored from a two year old backup tape. He no longer remembered what the password had been. His former IT guy had never documented the password. When the client notified us, we immediately went to their archive documentation and pulled the password that was active at that time because we had documented their network. We gave the password to the client, and they were able to login and complete the work that they were doing.

Network Passwords

Domain and Service Accounts

Domain	Login:	Administrator
	Password:	NotTelling!!!
Active Directory Restore	Login:	Administrator
	Password:	NotTelling!!!
Virus Protection	Login:	svcAVProtect
	Password:	NotTelling!!!

Application logins

Backup Software	Login:	BUSVCADMIN
	Password:	NotTelling!!!

Hardware logins

Router - _____

Login:	admin
Password:	NotTelling!!!
Telnet Password:	admin
Full Access Password:	NotTelling!!!

Firewall - _____

Login:	admin
Password:	NotTelling!!!
Telnet Password:	admin
Full Access Password:	NotTelling!!!

Figure 19 – Example Network Password Form

> **Tip:** *you may want to keep the master password sheet offsite, in a secure location. For copies kept at the office, I recommend that you keep it in a locked drawer, cabinet, or somewhere secure. Network electronic copies should be kept in a directory file structure that has limited access, perhaps only the Domain Administrators will have permissions to open or edit the doc.*
>
> *Do not just print and put in a binder and then leave it lying around.*

Firewall Configuration

I encounter clients all the time who simply believe that by having a firewall installed between the Internet and their network that their network will be secure. This false sense of security creates havoc when a network is breached, and brings upon the onset of learning that being secure today does not mean that you are secure tomorrow.

Understanding how your firewall is configured and documenting it properly is important, not just for being able to identify the potential threats of security holes for gaps and configuration issues but also for troubleshooting. This helps us understand how traffic should flow inbound and out, as well as what ports or pin holes are opened through it. Imagine one of those IQ tests that have the different shaped holes in it. Picture it as big as the door to your office. Now picture it as the door to your office if the door was shut. If there were no handle or hinges, you could not just walk into the next room, could you?

This is, in essence, how a firewall works. It blocks most traffic, but you open up different shaped holes so that people can put things through them if they have objects of the right shape. If you have a firewall and have configured it properly, you may have opened up one or more "holes" in it. Email and web services being two of the most common holes opened up through a firewall. Email works on port 25 and web services on port 80. If you think of email as a block, and web traffic as a circle, there will have to be a hole in the firewall to let it pass through to the inside of the network, and the firewall will have to know who gets the block or circle. If you did not open up the port for email, then the email block would never pass to the inside of the network.

There are many types of firewalls, each of which may have different kinds of interfaces, or configuration methods to login and configure the device. Unfortunately, there is not a standard for documenting a firewall that will fully document every kind out there.

I will cover basic documentation that will be common to all of the firewalls, but I will leave it to you to add the additional information to make your firewall management easier. The data that you collect will be useful, and in many cases all that you need to troubleshoot or to configure a new replacement device in the event of equipment failure.

Step one is to document the user name and passwords for the device, IP address information, and the warranty/technical support options. Step two is to map out what ports are open on the outside and on the inside interfaces. Lastly you will document the remaining configuration of the device. If you have a Cisco PIX firewall, then you would want to copy the text based configuration file for the documentation. If you have a device that does not have the ability to export the configuration in a readable format, like a device that only has a graphical interface, then you may need to do screenshots of the configuration. You may want to expand on this document to capture the fields relating to the configuration.

I would strongly encourage that you make a backup of the firewall's configuration direct from the appliance. Most firewall and router manufacturers provide a method for creating and archiving a binary image of the configuration file. This should be copied to your server and backed up offsite. Often, this provides for a fast recovery using the binary image to restore functionality to either a replacement device, or to itself in the event of a lost configuration, or a mis-configuration of the device.

General Information – The top section of the form is used for collecting specific data such as the make and model, serial number, firmware and Operating System information of the firewall. In addition, we want to capture the warranty and support information including the expiration of support. This is important to track as most devices have renewable warranties on their equipment, but if it expires, many have long waiting periods for it to be reactivated. This means that you do not want to find out that your warranty expired last month and that you may have to wait 90 days to get it back under support during an outage or when it is broken.

Once you have collected this information, please remember to keep it updated when you perform service and updates to the equipment and its configuration.

Access Rules – This section documents the way traffic is analyzed to determine whether or not to allow it to pass through the firewall. Like a traffic cop, it manages the flow or is the gatekeeper. Most firewalls process its rules from allowed to denied with deny rules being last. If you configure your firewall to allow all traffic and a later rule to deny all traffic, guess what, all traffic is going to get passed through the firewall. As you document these rules, you will want to review them to ensure that only the appropriate traffic is being passed through. This includes reviewing both inbound (outside in) and outbound (inside out) access rules.

On the following form, the Access Rules section is setup to allow you to list the following; the service name, the IP port, the protocol (TCP, UDP, both), is it allowed or denied, and the direction of access. Source IP is the "From" and Destination IP is the "To" address.

For example: An allow rule with a source of Any, and a destination to a Private IP address would allow all traffic from the outside that is directed to that port to pass thru the firewall to the designated IP address. For this to work, there will have to be a NAT/PAT rule mapping the public IP address to this private IP address.

You will need to analyze all the firewall rules in order to complete this table. Typically, this table will need more lines to complete. If you have a complex environment, this may take several pages to complete for just one firewall. Do not feel overwhelmed if this is your first firewall to document. You will find that in a multi-site environment, the primary network has the most complicated set of rules, and that the remote sites have very few rules.

64

Often, the remote sites or locations, do not have inbound access opened up, especially if there are no servers at the remote site. Do not let this fool you, audit every firewall in your network and you may be surprised at what you find.

NAT/PAT – NAT stands for Network Address Translations and PAT stands for Port Address Translation. PAT is a type of NAT. This allows you to utilize a public IP address on the outside and "Map" it to a private IP address on the inside. Private IP addresses are not routable over the Internet, so to limit risk, most companies do not put their servers totally on the outside the firewall. By utilizing NAT/PAT you are able to limit the exposure to the Internet, and further reduce the security risk. In addition, you can utilize the same public IP address and have different service ports point to different internal IP addresses. For example, email (port 25) could go to server x.x.x.5 and www (port 80) could go to server x.x.x.7, and so on.

On the firewall configuration form, the NAT/PAT section should be completed as well. Here is where you write down the rules for what is mapped between each external IP address and the internal IP address. A word of caution, sometimes the ports are mapped differently, as in, port 80 on the external IP address may be mapped to port 8088 on an inside (internal) IP address. It is important to understand what each port is and the role that it plays. In addition, you need to identify whether the port is still required and active in the environment.

I have split this table so that it is easy to read left to right. We start with the external IP address and port number. If the mail record for your domain pointed to a public IP address on your firewall, then you would write down the public IP address and port 25. The description would be similar to SMTP or Email service. I usually use the technical port annotation. I would put "SMTP" as the description. Then I would put the Internal IP address that this is mapped to along with the port number. In this case, port 25, as this is the port on the mail server that it maps too.

Firewall Configuration

Make and Model _____

Serial Number: _____

Warranty/Support Contract#: _____

Start Date: _____ **End Date:** _____ **Renewable?** _____

Firmware Version _____ **Revision:** _____

OS/IOS Version _____ **Revision:** _____

Support Contact: _____

Contract Information/Password: _____

LAN/Internal IP		WAN/External IP		Security	
IP		IP		User Name:	
SN		SN			
GW		GW		Password:	
IP		IP			

Access Rules

Service name	Port #:	Protocol(s):	Access	Source IP:	Destination IP:
(example) HTTP	80	TCP	Allow	Any	10.10.10.10
SMTP (Email)	25				
HTTPS (WEB)	443				
RDP/TS	3389				

NAT/PAT

External IP address	Ports	Description	Internal IP	Ports

Figure 20 – Firewall Configuration Form

> **TIP:** _Always backup the firewall configurations to disk. I prefer to backup the configurations up to a server into an IT directory that is secured as well as backed up. In addition, I usually archive these files to a CD or DVD along with other specialty files, like device drivers, firmware patches, etc._

Chapter 5 – Network Information

Network Quick Reference

The Network Quick Reference is a great place for keeping a summary of frequently used information. This template has many of the most common items that we use daily with our clients. This is a part of the document that you will want to make sure is always up to date, and easily available.

You will want to keep important items like key passwords, IP addresses, tech support numbers and support contract information here. In addition, other information like domain registration and warranty expirations, network domain information such as key printers, file shares and domain information are also good to keep up with here in this section. The example covered here, is to get you started. Feel free to add more sections to this summary based upon what is most important in your network environment.

The information contained in this section is not a complete picture. This is the cheat sheet for your critical data that you utilize frequently on a day to day basis, more detailed information is captured in other areas of the documentation.

Network Quick Reference

Company Name:

ISP Name	abcIISP
Tech Support Phone:	
Circuit Id/Account #	
Telco Name	abcIISP
Tech Support Phone:	
Circuit Id/Account #	

Router IP	Xxxxxxxxxx
Router User/PW)	
Telnet (User/PW)	xx.xxxx.xxx.xxx
URL:	Https://xxxxxxxxx
Notes:	
Local IP Address Range:	

Figure 21 – Network Quick Reference Example

Contracts, Warranties and License Information

Use this form for capturing a summary of items that need to be renewed annually, or periodically. Many of these may have greater detail in its respective documentation section. If necessary, use a second line for additional information. Generally speaking, use one line per item. This is a summary page to allow you to keep all those items that will expire to be centralized in one place. The benefit that this brings is to have a single reference to keep track of all those expirations and renewals. If you think it is overly redundant to keep a document of this type up to date with the two summary sections included, I would challenge that you probably have never had the pleasure to find out at 2am in the morning amidst troubleshooting a network outage that a support contract expired two weeks ago.

Information to collect on this form includes items such as: the vendor or reseller name, the type of contract or license, what device the license covers and the start and end dates of coverage. It is good to notate whether it is a renewable warranty or license as well. That way, if it is not renewable, you can determine or plan the replacement strategy or support strategy in case it fails. It is good to start the renewal process at least 60 days in advance. There are times when a vendor discontinues support on a product line. When you encounter this scenario, you will need time to begin planning on what to do when that equipment fails. Your support strategy may be to continue use the device till it fails or it may be time to plan on replacing the equipment while it is still in production and working fine. Regardless of the method that you select, knowing in advance is always better than finding out when the equipment has failed and you are not able to receive the support to get it back in operation.

I would recommend that you review this sheet at least once every month to review and plan for renewals and replacements.

Contracts, Warranties and License Information

Vendor	Type	Device	Start Date	Expiration
XYZ Vendor	HW Support	Firewall	01-01-2008	12-31-2008
DNS Registrar	Domain Name	<domainname>	N/A	07-24-2010

Figure 22 –Example Contracts, & License Information

Software License & Install Key Information

This is a simple form for collecting the software license information and install code(s) or product key(s) for each application on a server or workstation. One form should be used for each computer in the network. I recommend starting with the servers as this impacts all of the users.

The vendor is the manufacturer or software developer of the software.

Type is where you will want to identify each application by type of program or the business function that is serves. You might describe the type of application with simple descriptive names such as accounting, operating system, email server and office productivity, etc.

The install key or product code is the code that is utilized or supplied during the installation of the software. Some applications may have multiple keys or codes to be installed in order to add or configure additional functions or modules. For applications requiring multiple product keys, you may capture on multiple lines in the document.

The notes section you will use to write down custom or additional information for an application or for additional software installation instructions. This might include custom install directories, or special tasks that need to be completed to reinstall an application. Other information might include ODBC (database) connections, server names and settings for setting up the client side of an application after the initial install.

You may find that some applications require extensive configurations prior to it being ready for a specific user or department. You will need to document these additional steps to ensure that you will be able to install or re-install the application properly.

Software License & Install Key Information

Computer:		
Vendor	**Type**	**Install Key/Code**

Notes:

Figure 23 – Software License & Key Information

Key Device Information

Let's refer to the simple network diagram that you drew out at the beginning of this project. You will identify all the key components that are not servers, and organize them by type. You will gather the appropriate information for each device that will be utilized to support and understand the network environment.

Devices that you will usually document in this section typically include IP based devices such as routers, firewalls, network switches, server room UPS batteries, Power Distribution Units (PDU), KVM appliances and network printers. For each device you will gather the make and model information, serial number, and the IP address information. In addition, we want to fill out where the device is located at the facility. For wireless routers and access points this can be more critical, as these are often located out of sight. When these devices have issues, it is good to know exactly where to go find them.

If there is a warranty on the device, then you will also need to document this additional information. Just like routers and firewalls, other devices on your network most likely have renewable warranties too. This is beneficial for technical support and upgrades to those devices. Many vendors release firmware and software updates that are only available under an active support contract. If you do not have support contracts on these devices you will want to spend some time analyzing and determine whether or not to pursue obtaining one.

Key Device Information

Router

        Make and Model: _____

        S/N: _____

        External IP Address: _____

        Internal IP Address: _____

        Location: _____

        Warranty Info: _____

Firewall

        Make and Model: _____

        S/N: _____

        External IP Address: _____

        Internal IP Address: _____

        Location: _____

        Warranty Info: _____

Ethernet Switch1

        Make and Model: _____

        Type: _____

        S/N: _____

        External IP Address: _____

        Internal IP Address: _____

        Location: _____

        Internal IP Address: _____

        Warranty Info: _____

Ethernet Switch2

        Make and Model: _____

        Type: _____

        S/N: _____

        Location: _____

        Warranty Info: _____

Figure 24 – Key Device Information Form

Printer Information

There are several key points regarding the documentation of printers. Depending on how the network is configured the printer could be a networked, shared, or a stand-alone printer.

A stand-alone printer is typically connected directly to a workstation and only that one workstation is setup to use.

A shared printer could reside directly on the network or connected locally (directly) to the computer that is hosting the shared printer.

A networked printer is typically connected to the network via an Ethernet cable, or using a print server device that connects to the network via Ethernet but may only connect to the printer via USB or parallel interfaces.

Typical information that you will want collect includes:

- Device IP info
- Warranty /maintenance agreements
- Consumables/Part numbers
- Special notes:
- Print driver information, version, and where to download.

Printer Form Example

Make and Model: _____

Serial Number: _____

Warranty/Support Contract#: _____

Start Date: _____ **End Date:** _____ **Renewable?** _____

Firmware Version _____ **Revision:** _____

Support Contact: _____

Contract Information/Password: _____

Management IP/URL: _____

Login: (User Name/Password) _____

Network IP: _____

Shared Name: _____

Host Server: _____

Driver Name: _____

Network Path To Install File: _____

Consumables		
Description	MFG PN	Preferred Vendor
Black toner		
Cyan		
Magenta		
Yellow		
Imaging Drum		

Figure 25 – Printer Information Form

Power Distribution Devices

The Power Distribution Unit or PDU for short is a common device to have that the servers and infrastructure plug into. A managed PDU is a good investment as it allows you to remotely power cycle a device such as a server or router that is not responding. Especially useful for late night reboots or issues that require you to manually pull the plug on the power. With a remote or managed PDU, you can remotely connect and schedule a hard power cycle. This is great for late night restarts or hung servers as this lets you quickly handle a power cycle without having to go pull the cable manually.

Typical information that you will want collect includes:

- Location
- Make//model/etc like key device info
- IP addresses for management
- User/pw
- Port info
- What is connected to each port
- Special instructions

TIP: It is good practice to document the startup order of the servers as well as any dependencies for startup.

This will allow you to schedule or sequence the power down and power on of devices in the correct order.

PDU Form Example

Make and Model: _____ __ of __

Serial Number: _____

Location/Rack: _____

Warranty/Support Contract#: _____

Start Date: _____   End Date: _____   Renewable? _____

Firmware Version _____   Revision: _____

Support Contact: _____

Contract Information/Password: _____

Management IP/URL: _____

User Name: _____

Password:

Special Notes:

Ports	Description
1	
2	
3	
4	
5	
6	
7	
8	

Figure 26 – PDU Device Information Form

KVM Switch Information

The Keyboard/Video/Monitor switch is most often referred to as a KVM. The KVM allows a user to utilize a single monitor, keyboard and mouse to access multiple computers one at a time. This is different than remote access to a computer as the keyboard, mouse, and monitor are all local and directly attached via the switch to the computers. This allows you to save space in a server room or server rack, by only requiring one monitor, one keyboard and one mouse to control many devices. If there is more than one server, I believe it is well worth the investment to deploy a KVM.

Documenting a KVM correctly is very important. If the KVM has programmable onscreen options it is good to keep it updated as well. Many KVM devices utilize keyboard shortcut hot keys or physical buttons on the device itself to switch its connection between attached computers. Many of the manufacturers setup password protection that requires you to know the password. So this will be important for you to check as you document this section and capture the username and password if available.

Typical information that you will want collect includes:

- Location
- Make//model/etc like key device info
- IP addresses for management
- User/pw
- Key press combination
- Port info
- What is connected to each port
- Special instructions

KVM Form Example

Make and Model: _____ __ of __

Serial Number: _____

Location/Rack: _____

Warranty/Support Contract#: _____

Start Date: _____ End Date: _____ Renewable? _____

Firmware Version _____ Revision: _____

Support Contact: _____

Contract Information/Password: _____

Management IP/URL: _____	Cable set type/PN:
User Name: _____	
Password:	

Special Notes:

Ports	Description
1	
2	
3	
4	
5	
6	
7	
8	

Figure 27 – KVM Device Information Form

80

Computer Summary Details

The forms in this section are designed to document the basic configuration of a single computer in the network environment. This will let you build a summary page for each server, workstation and laptop in the environment. This should be updated when any changes are made to the systems. I recommend documenting individual PC's asset/service tag and serial number information as well as the lease expiration and service information. This will help ensure that if service is required, then the warranty information can be identified rapidly.

In auditing individual computers, it is best practice to identify the non-standard or custom hardware and the associated software drivers that are required. If the PC ever has to be rebuilt or have the operating system reloaded, then these drivers will be required in order to successfully recover the computer. A handy way to keep up with these special drivers is to 'burn" or copy them to a CD and keep it with the software for each PC. Keeping track of all the software for a computer in a central location is a good idea, especially if you organize and label a package for each PC. This way, in the event that you need to perform a reload or upgrade, all you will have to do is pull the PC's software library and you are ready to go. This saves time hunting down missing installation CD/DVD media, drivers and files, so that you or the IT staff can complete the task at hand quickly and efficiently.

Typical information that you will want collect includes:

- CPU (qty, speed, manufacturer)
  - Example: 2 x Intel P4 3.6Ghz
- RAM
- Hard drives
- Network card
- Chassis Type
- Vendor/Manufacturer
- Serial number
- Asset tag/service tag
- Warranty #/Expiration/Contact information
- Lease Information/Expiration
- Custom Information

I usually include the CD (or backup copy) and the product/install keys for all the installed software. If volume license keys are utilized, then I usually notate a reference to the volume license information rather than the actual key. It does not hurt to document the actual volume key for each computer on this form. However, I recommend that you remain consistent throughout your documentation. Consistency brings about standardization, and a standardized documentation process is what you are building.

Computer Details Form

Computer Name: _____

Vendor: _____   Chassis: _____

Serial Number: _____   Asset Tag: _____

Lease Expiration: _____

Warranty Info: _____

Operating System: _____   Service Pack: _____

Virus Protection: _____   Expiration: _____

Hardware Configuration:			
CPU:	Memory:	Video	Backup Device
# Hard Drives:	Network Card	Modem:	RAID Controller

Hard Drive:	Vol. Name:	Part. Size	Used Space:	Free Space:

Local Printers, Devices, Peripherals:

Application :	Key:

Notes:

Figure 28 – Computer Details Form

PC Summary Table

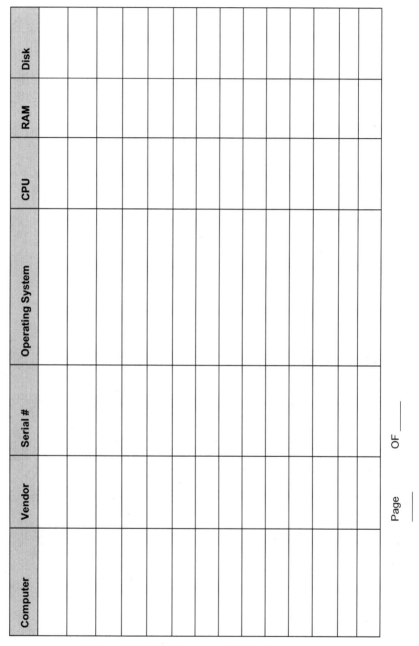

Figure 29 – PC Summary Table Form

Chapter 6 – Network and Domain

File and Print Shares

Through the years, I have found that many questions asked by users when they have a problem relate to file and print share mapping. These type of support questions are often repetitive general network 'how do I' type of questions. Many of these questions include aspects of the network for what printer they connect to, or a user deleted their drive mapping, and needs to know what folder to connect their drive letter.

Users often know that they save files to the G drive or the H drive although they do not know where those drives are located. When a user calls support and say that they lost their H drive, knowing where that drive letter is supposed to be mapped makes responding that much faster. When you do not know, you may have to ask the user for specific file names and then search each server to find the file and the directory where it is located.

Network File Shares – This table shows the general network shares that users and applications utilize. It is important to document these as they are typically utilized across the network.

The following list describes the fields that should be completed:

- **Server** – list the server name where the shared resource is located.

- **Share Name** – List the actual name of the shared resource. File shares ending with a $ do not show up in Network Browsing. They are called a hidden share.

- **Directory Path** – Capture the actual file system level path to the shared folder. Begin with the physical drive letter and follow to the final folder that is shared. Do not put the sub folders after the share point. If you have to recreate the share, you will create the share at the wrong location.

- **Permissions** – There are two types of permissions, file level and share level permissions. Since we are documenting shares, we want to list the share level permissions, meaning which users and groups have access to this share. Microsoft follows the most restrictive path for file and share permissions. If a user has write permissions on the share, but has read only permissions at the directory or file level, then that user will not be able to write files to this directory.

Home Directory – This table is to show where a user's home directory is located. If you have a complex network or have users home directories on multiple servers, then you will need document all of these. You may need to show what users are connected to which server home directory. The field descriptions are the same as the standard network file shares.

Network IP Printers – Next we will detail the network printer shares. It is good to review this list after it is completed. You will want to look for duplicate printer configurations and incorrect printer device types.

File and Print Shares

Network File Shares

Server	Share Name	Directory Path	Permissions

Network IP Printers

Server	Share Name	IP Address	Printer Type

Home Directory Information

Server	Share Name	Directory Path

Figure 30 – File & Print Share Form

WINS

WINS is a service Microsoft implemented as in interim solution until DDNS was approved and the RFC process was completed. WINS is a legacy service and is no longer needed with a full Windows 2000/2003 Active Directory implementation. Once complete this service can be removed, according to Microsoft. The reality is that there are more than just legacy applications that still rely upon WINS for name resolution across the network. At this time, I still recommend that WINS be installed on the network domain unless you are running a pure, up to date, Microsoft platform end to end with only the latest and greatest Microsoft applications. Otherwise, you might spend more time than you would like troubleshooting legacy applications.

In this template, I recommend using one section for each server that has WINS installed. In the purpose field you should write out, or list, the legacy applications that require the use of WINS. This way when you review or look at removing WINS from the network, you will be able to identify the legacy applications to research to see whether they have an upgrade path or version that no longer requires this service.

WINS

Server Name:	
Item	Description
IP Address	
Purpose	
Replication Configuration	

Figure 31 – WINS Form

DHCP

DHCP is a network service that assigns IP addresses and other information used to configure the network cards of devices automatically. Other services include default gateways, subnet masks, DNS and WINS servers, router information, time servers, and many other items. DHCP is preferred for larger networks due to the ease of centralized management. It allows administrators to manage the network configuration settings with less headache and frustration than by managing hard coded or static IP addresses. With DHCP, an administrator can make changes to the IP addressing scheme used on a network, without having to touch each individual workstation and device. Routers, switches, printers and firewalls are typically configured with a static IP address although you may find reservations for devices that have semi-static IP addresses. That means the device uses DHCP but the DHCP server always assigns the same IP address over and over. This lets you still have the flexibility of centralized management and have the consistency of a static address. This also helps to reduce the potential of having duplicate static IP addresses assigned on a network.

DHCP

Server Name:	
Item	**Description**
IP Address	
Scope	
Exclusions	
Options	

Figure 32 – DHCP Form

89

DNS

The DNS Server service is a key application for Active Directory domains. This service is the primary means to identify IP Addresses to host names and domain services. In addition, the DNS Server may be configured to host additional information for other domain names, commonly referred to as DNS zones. In documenting the DNS services it is good to review each DNS server to identify additional domains as well as replication between the DNS servers.

DNS

Server Name:	
Item	**Description**
IP Address	
Forward Lookup Zones	
Forward Lookup Zone Type	
Reverse Lookup Zone	
Reverse Lookup Zone Type	
Manually configured hosts	

Figure 33 – DNS Information Form

TIP: There are many Visual Basic scripts that can assist in pulling this information rapidly. Many of these can be coded to show the results in a format that can be cut and pasted into your documentation

Local DNS Host Record Sheet

Domain Name: _____

Host/Node	Type (A, CName, MX)	IP address (Public)
Example: Mail.<YourDomainNAme.com>	MX 10	Aaa.bbb.ccc.ddd

Figure 34 – DNS Host Records Form

Active Directory Domain Information

In this section, you are going to gather key data regarding the network domain. This information is important for day to day administration and for troubleshooting. The following form covers basic information regarding Active Directory. The Active directory Domain name is the fully qualified Domain name. Typically this will be similar to 'yourdomainname.local'. This will be the full DNS name of the internal network domain.

The NetBIOS name is the friendly, or short, name that is used for the domain. No, not the nickname that you give the network, but the short name that is actually configured.

The Domain admin account is the network Domain level administrator account, not the local server administrator. In addition, the Active Directory Restore password is important to document. This password is used during a system state restore or Active Directory restoration. You will be unable to perform this type of restore without the password. If this password is not known, then you will most likely need to recreate or reset this password. When you do, document it! Otherwise you will not be able to restore Active Directory to your server.

Global Catalog (GC) servers are servers that provide additional information to the network for Active Directory, and allow changes to be made to Active Directory. Global Catalog servers hold complete copies of the Active Directory schema.

Capturing which servers are email servers helps to understand the topology of how email traffic flows across the network. Later, you will define the roles that each server provides for the network and you will document the email role, such as front end or back end email server. For now, we are identifying which server has MS Exchange server services installed.

If you have a multiple site environment, you most likely have configured Active Directory sites. AD Sites allow traffic from a specific IP address range to find the closest Domain Controller for authentication and general Active Directory traffic. This helps improve network performance if requests can be handled on the local network instead of being passed across the Internet, VPN, or slower WAN traffic connections.

The last part of the following form is to capture the Flexible Single Master Operations (FSMO) roles. Initially, these are installed on the first Domain Controller or DC in the domain. In larger environments, these roles are typically separated out across multiple domain servers. If these roles are not active, such as being on a server that is removed from the domain, then you will need to 'seize' the roles. I've included a visual basic script that you can utilize that will help you to quickly identify which server holds each role. If a server is identified that is no longer on the network, then you have an action item to track down.

Active Directory Domain Information

Item	Description
Active Directory Domain:	
NetBIOS Domain Name	
Domain Admin Account	
AD Restore Password	
Domain Controllers:	
Global Catalogue Servers:	
MS Exchange Server	

Active Directory Sites

Site Name:	Location	IP Range	Subnet

FSMO Roles

Role	Active Directory Location
Schema Master	
Domain Naming Master	
RID Master	
PDC Emulator	
Infrastructure Master	

Figure 35 – Key Active Directory Components

Server Roles

This form is designed to capture a short summary describing the server's purpose or business function. The server role is simply identifying what each server does or provides for the network. This is where you will identify network domain services such as DNS, DHCP, email, databases, customer and key applications. I recommend that you summarize by key role and then expand with a little more detail in plain English. This is where you can really start describing what each server does for the environment. You might find that you have a lot of services or tasks being performed or very few on a server by server basis.

The IIS (Internet Information Service) is Microsoft's Web server. As you audit and document your network, you will need to open the IIS management console and identify what web sites are installed and active. Documenting the web services, directory location, and other key data, will help to identify and maintain these web sites or services. If you ever decommission a server, this will help you to ensure that you are able to move the website and be able to bring it up online somewhere else.

Routing and remote access is where you will document the remote availability for end users. The remote access method and information that should be documented may not be on the servers. Many times, these services may be configured on an infrastructure device such as a router or firewall. Sometimes there may be many connections from the outside to the network. Remember to also look for old fashioned ways of accessing the network, like a dial up modem. They are still out there, often to the chagrin of the IT manager.

As you review the network, you will most likely speak to executives or department managers in addition to technical staff. Do not be afraid to ask questions on what kind of connectivity or applications that they use outside of the office.

Server Roles

Server Name	Roles in Network
Example: Server01	*DC, DNS, DHCP, Exchange*

IIS

Item	Description
Version	
InetPub Location	
Purpose	
Security	
Frontpage Extensions	

Routing and Remote Access

Item	Description
Remote Access Ports	
Remote Access Security	
Remote Access Policy Specs	
IP Assigned Via	
Routing Purpose	
NAT Configuration	

Figure 36 – Key Server Roles Form

MS SQL Database Information

Databases are an important part of your network. There are many places that databases reside, and more and more applications are implementing databases as part of their software. Data, data everywhere you look. You will need to review each instance of the database services to identify what databases are there and what applications require them.

This is especially true if you are running MS SharePoint or other applications that explicitly rely upon them. It will also be necessary to identify if there other scheduled tasks that have to run that might create reports, modify or move data from one Database to another at a minimum.

Reviewing SQL scripts, stored procedures and tasks is important to the documentation process as well. Scripts and tasks have programming code that may need to be documented. If there are custom databases, then you will have to create more detailed documentation. This may already be available by the developer. If so, that is awesome. If not, then you will need to document this. There are many tools to assist with this as well as, numerous scripts that can be used to document other necessary SQL management and documentation functions.

MS SQL Database information forms

MS SQL SERVER INFORMATION			
Server:			
Product:		Version:	
Startup Parameters:			
Security:		Audit Level:	
Instance Name:			
SA User / PW			

Login Name	PW	Database assigned	Roles/Rights

DATABASES			
Name:		Compat. Level:	
DB File/Path			Size:
LOG File/Path			Size:
DATABASES			
Name:		Compat. Level:	
DB File/Path			Size:
LOG File/Path			Size:
DATABASES			
Name:		Compat. Level:	
DB File/Path			Size:
LOG File/Path			Size:

Figure 37 –MS SQL Server Form

Email Configuration

This overview is a wordy, high level description that should describe where the Email servers are located in the network, how users access their email such as via Outlook Web Access, RPC over HTTP, OutlookAnyWhere or the standard MS Outlook client. I recommend that you also list which server(s) are front end email servers and which are backend servers.

Microsoft Exchange Server Installation

This section is for documenting key information relating to the MS Exchange Server installation. This information is useful and most of the information is required to perform a recovery of the email server. Although much of this information is stored in Active Directory, there are several key pieces of information that is required to manage, script, as well as be able to rebuild a failed MS Exchange Server environment. The majority of this information can be found rapidly via the MS Exchange System administration console.

The following describes what data is captured:

Organization (Org name) – The organization name is the top level name of the Exchange directory structure.

Site Name – There may be multiple physical sites in the network but this section is for the logical email sites. They will be represented as distinct sites under the Exchange architecture. Each site should be listed.

Email Host Alias – For every email server, the Host alias should be documented. This is the name that the server represents itself to the network and the Internet when it sends emails.

Computer Name – This is the network host name of the server. If you have multiple servers in the email environment, then you will need to list all of them here.

Service Account and Password – It is recommended to create a dedicated Exchange service account. It is best practice to not use the

Domain Administrator account as the service account for MS Exchange. This will allow changes to the Domain administrator account to not impact the email server configuration.

Connectors – The MS Exchange system has the ability to have multiple connectors for sending and receiving email. The email connector allows different paths with different configurations to be utilized. For the MS Internet email filtering options to be utilized it must be configured at the connector level.

SMTP Domains – The primary SMTP domain is the default email address domain that is handled by the servers. Many corporate email servers handle multiple email domains for inbound and outbound email. Some of these may be sub domains and others may be standalone email domains.

OWA URL – This is the HTTP or HTTPS address that remote and local users utilize for accessing Outlook Web Access. This may be different internally than it is across the public Internet. In some cases, there may be multiple OWA servers in more complex or larger environments.

Free Disk Space – The free disk space of the hard drive volumes that hold the message store data files and transaction logs should be documented here. Microsoft recommends that at no time should the private information store of any Exchange server in the Organization be allowed to grow past 50% of available disk space. This provides adequate room for maintenance procedures (such as de-fragmentation) and future upgrades.

Maintenance Schedule – Based on the scheduled maintenance that is configured for each mail server, document the type of maintenance to be perform and its associated schedule. Every private and public database in the Exchange Organization should be checked for consistency and de-fragmented by normal Exchange maintenance routines. Exchange Server 2003 best practice is to never run Operating System level de-fragmentation utilities on hard drives containing the message store databases.

Component Location

Information Stores – We want to locate and write down where the message store and log files are located.

Tip – The Email host alias is important to have configured properly. In addition, as you audit the network environment you will need to compare against your internal and public DNS host records to ensure that the mail exchanger (MX) records are configured properly to match this alias.

Reverse DNS is commonly used to check for servers sending SPAM. This works by comparing the IP address of the sending email server and then seeing if it matches the Host name that is sending the email. Reverse DNS is usually handled with your Telco/ISP provider. If you do not have static public IP addresses for your email server, you will most likely have issues sending email to many of your customers or prospects.

Email Configuration Example

The following tables shows an example of a completed form:

Overview

ABC Company utilizes a front end/back end server configuration with multiple back end servers. SERVER01 is the primary back end mail server that holds the majority of user mailboxes. SERVER02 holds the executive mailboxes and WEB01 is the front end mail server as well as hosts the OWA services.

Microsoft Exchange Server Installation

Item	Data
Org name	ABC Company Org
Site name	Default First Site
Email Host Alias	
Computer name	SERVER01
Service account	Exchange_SVC
Service account password	Not-telling-you
Connectors	
Primary SMTP domain	EMaildomain.com
Additional SMTP Domains	Email2.com
OWA URL	http://YourDomainName.com/Exchange
Free Disk Space (%)	50%
Maintenance Schedule	Online maintenance: 1am - 5am

Figure 38 –MS Exchange Server Form

Email Component Location

Component Location

Component	Location
Private information store (.edb)	\exchsrvr\mdbdata
Private information store (.stm)	\exchsrvr\mdbdata
Public information store (.edb)	\exchsrvr\mdbdata
Public information store(.stm)	\exchsrvr\mdbdata
Information store logs	\exchsrvr\mdbdata
Directory service	\exchsrvr\dsadata
Directory service logs	\exchsrvr\dsadata
Message transfer agent	\exchsrvr\mtadata
Internet Mail Service files	Exchsrvr\imcdata
Key Management Server files	\exchsrvr\kmsdata

Notes:

Figure 39 –Email Components Form

Backup Information

Network backups, need I say more? "I need to get an important report restored from last night's backup!" I can just hear half of you cringe at that statement. Backing up the network is a key function of IT support as well as being highly critical to the business. Recoverability of the business information and data is of prime importance. If you were to lose all the data for a business that could potentially put them out of business. The responsibility of IT is not just to have a backup system that says it backed up files but to have a proven backup strategy.

When was the last time you performed a test restore from a backup set? I would venture a guess and say that you were not sure. Do you remember the last time that you looked at what is actually being backed up or confirmed that the system state has been backed up? Do you periodically review what is configured to be backed up and compare this to changes that have been made to the network?

I feel that this is one of the more important sections to double check during this audit. In order to perform a data restore, during a disaster recovery scenario, it is important to know the type of tape drive, backup software version, and what was backed up.

Hardware – This section is used to detail the type of tape drive or backup device, model and manufacturer of the device. If the device is an autoloader, then we need to capture the information on this hardware in addition to the actual installed tape drive. Many newer backup devices do not utilize tape based media but other types such as removable hard drive cartridges.

The software driver and firmware version is important to track down and capture. Some backup devices require that you have the same version of the driver as was in use during the actual backup. It is recommended to keep the firmware and software updated to the latest versions.

Software – The software version and type of backup software should be captured in this section. The software version and hot fix levels should be kept updated. The Job Configuration section describes how this backup solution is configured in your environment and should describe the media rotation schedule.

The details of what is backed up and which day the job runs should be completed. I would recommend that you refer to this list monthly (at a minimum) and confirm that everything that should be backed up is being backed up successfully.

The rotation schedule is used to help manage when a particular piece of media should be installed and how the rotation of tapes should be handled. This grid can also be expanded for end-users who change tapes to know which tape should be put in each day.

Backup Solution

Hardware

Hardware	Description
Tape Drive	
AutoLoader	
Driver version	
Updated/Firmware	

Software

Software	Description
Backup Software	
Version	
Responsibilities	
Day of Week	**Backup Job Details**
Monday	
Tuesday	
Wednesday	
Thursday	
Friday	
Saturday	
Sunday	

Tape Rotation

Sun	Mon	Tue	Wed	Thu	Fri	Sat

Figure 40 –Backup Solution Form

Appendix

In your network audit book this section will be utilized for general information, additional details, and other items as you identify them. This is where I usually put copies of login scripts, batch files and especially copies of the router and firewall configuration files. These are typically long, multiple page text files.

A key section that I put here, or in a secondary book based upon the size of the network, is the computer summaries of the servers and workstations. The summary usually includes all the basic information about the computer hardware, and some basic information such as the IP address and subnet ranges. The computer summaries are good information to have but information that may not be needed as frequently. The purpose of this book is to have quick access to the information that you need on a daily and weekly basis.

I also like to keep images of all the installation media for a server in CD protector sleeves either in this section or depending on the number of disks in a dedicated CD carrying case. You will want to include the installation product keys and the computer name that each is assigned for easy reference. This will allow you to keep the originals safe and secure.

Login Scripts

Network administrators have many ways and methods available for them to manage user settings. These tools can range from simple command line batch files to complex scripts using specialized scripting languages. Two of the more common scripting languages used for this purpose include KiXtart and Visual Basic scripts. With the introduction of Windows Server 2008, Microsoft has released its newest scripting language standard, PowerShell. This will become the new standard for Microsoft management scripting. New technologies, such as Windows Server 2008, MS Exchange 2007 and MS SQL 2005/2008 include PowerShell scripts to perform general management and configuration tasks   Login scripts come in many flavors. Some are as simple as mapping a drive letter to a network share for every user while others may be very complex.

There may be multiple login scripts in use depending upon the business requirements and network configuration. Some of these scripts may call other scripts to perform functions.

I recommend that you diagram out a work flow on the more complex scripts to help in troubleshooting them. For example, if a user in the accounting department needs access to a certain printer and file share, then the login script may compare the user name to active directory to check if the user is in the accounting department group. If so, then the login script may call a script called accounting and then map the printer and file share for that user. If the user is not in the accounting group, then it would not call or execute the accounting script.

In this section, I generally start a new page with each script unless I am able to fit two scripts entirely on the same page. I do not place a second script on the tail end of a multiple page script.

One of the simplest ways to begin is to go to the net logon share of the first Domain Controller and review the files that you find. I usually open them up in Notepad and then will cut and paste the file into the documentation. I use the file title as the title for each script and format it with the Heading Three format. If you are using the master template on the CD then you each script will then be listed in the table of contents appropriately thereby making it easy to find in a pinch.

If you have multiple locations, you may have different scripts in use at each remote site. A default printer for the main office may not be the default printer at the remote sites. This is important identify as you audit. Often the main scripts have been modified for the remote sites so you will need to review each script carefully for nuances. Do not just read the comments, as previous network administrators may not have changed the comments if they modified the script for a remote location. Just like documenting a network, documenting scripts often moves to a lower priority in an effort to get the job done. I personally take great pains to document the scripts that I develop, especially in our environment. Frequently, another engineer will be responsible for making updates and changes to the scripts. Without proper documentation in the scripts it makes it harder to keep up with what the script is supposed to accomplish.

Forms and Templates

This section is where I have included copies of most of the blank forms and templates that you can copy and use to get started. If you have purchased the documentation toolkit then you have the electronic edition of these forms and scripts on the included CD. I like the electronic versions of the forms so that I may type and edit as necessary, and then print a fresh, clean set of documentation. This eliminates the messiness of marking through or erasing information and then writing over it, as well as having to rewrite the whole page to clean it up.

If you have also purchased the full electronic toolkit then you already have the bonus database version which allows you to update and edit the information in the database, and then one click printing to print out a full copy of your network documentation.

I usually convert a copy of the documentation to a PDF version of the file and then store it in a secure location on the network with a password to minimize access. This ensures that the document may be printed on any printer.

The Book Tabs

This following is the list of the main tabs used in how I organized this book. You can customize each section and create your own sections for this book. You will probably add tabs later, even if you do not add or change the order today. The order of the tabs shown here is a guideline to help you get started.

- Overview
- General
- Telco
- General network
- Other

General Information

Contact List

Internal Contacts

Contact	Office	Home	Mobile	Email
*				
* Primary Technical Contacts				

Escalation Contacts

Contact	Office	Home	Mobile	Email
Desktop Support				
*				
Server Support				
*				
* Primary Technical Contacts				

Vendor Tech Support

Company	Contact	Office	Mobile	Email

Contract Number:
Notes:

Contract Number:
Notes:

Contract Number:
Notes:

Contract Number:
Notes:

Telco/ISP Contracts

Company	Contact	Office	Mobile	Email

Contract Number: Circuit ID:
Notes:

Contract Number: IP Address:
Notes:

Site Location Information

Site Name: _____   ___ Primary Site

Address: _____   **Primary Contact:**

_____   Name: _____

_____   Direct Phone: _____

_____   Home: _____

Office Phone: _____   Mobile: _____

Office Fax: _____   Email: _____

Notes:

Site Name: _____   ___ Primary Site

Address: _____   **Primary Contact:**

_____   Name: _____

_____   Direct Phone: _____

_____   Home: _____

Office Phone: _____   Mobile: _____

Office Fax: _____   Email: _____

Notes:

Network Overview

Network Summary

Network Diagram

Network Environment

Site Name: _____

Building Location of Key Equipment:

Location of Servers:

Security of the Server:

Lighting:

Condition of Cable:

Notes:

Network Security

Password Security

Length of Passwords:

Age of Passwords: _____

Computer Role _____

Domain Name _____

Primary Domain Controller _____

Forced Logoff Time _____

Min / Max Password Age _____

Minimum Password Length _____

Password History Length _____

Lockout Threshold _____

Lockout Duration _____

Lockout Observation Window _____

Network Security

Number of persons with administrator rights:

Admin Users List: _____

Is there a firewall in place? What type? _____

Server Room Security

Workstation Shares

Network Quick Reference

Company Name:

ISP Name

Tech Support Phone: _____

Circuit Id/Account # _____

Telco Name

Tech Support Phone: _____

Circuit Id/Account # _____

Router IP _____

Router User/PW) _____

Telnet (User/PW) _____

URL: _____

Notes:

Local IP Address Range:

Short information of key elements, passwords, and other useful information that is most commonly used goes here.

Telco Provider Information

Provider:	
Contract/Account #:	
Web URL:	
Web/Traffic URL:	
Admin Username:	
Password:	

Company	Contact	Office	Email

Contract Number:

Notes:

Circuit Information

Site Name	Type(DSL,T-1)	Circuit ID	Provider	Provisioned Equipment

Internet Service Provider Information

Provider:
Contract/Account #:
Web URL:
Web/Traffic URL:
Admin Username:
Password:

Company	Contact	Office	Email

Contract Number:
Notes:

Public IP Addresses

Site Name	IP Range	Def Gateway	Subnet	DNS1/DNS2

Domain Registration Form

Company/Organization: _____

Domain Name: _____

Last Updated:	__ / __ / __
Registration Expires:	__ / __ / __

Registrar:

Phone: _____

MGMT URL: _____

Admin Account: _____

Password: _____

Administrative Contact:

Email: _____

NIC Handle/User _____

Phone: _____

Technical Contact

Email: _____

NIC Handle/User _____

Phone: _____

Billing Contact

Email: _____

NIC Handle/User _____

Phone: _____

Primary DNS

Server Name: _____

IP Address _____

Secondary DNS

Server Name: _____

IP Address _____

Notes:

Public DNS Host Record Sheet

Domain Name:

Host/Node	Type (A, CName, MX)	IP address (Public)

Infrastructure Devices

Router Configuration

Make and Model _____

Serial Number: _____

Warranty/Support Contract#: _____

Start Date: _____ End Date: _____ Renewable? _____

Firmware Version _____ Revision: _____

OS/IOS Version _____ Revision: _____

Support Contact: _____

Contract Information/Password: _____

Telco Circuit ID: _____

PPPOE User _____

Password: _____

LAN/Internal IP		WAN/External IP		Security/Device
IP		IP		User Name:
SN		SN		
GW		GW		Password:
IP		IP		
DNS1		DNS1		
DNS2		DNS2		

Firewall Configuration

Make and Model _____

Serial Number: _____

Warranty/Support Contract#: _____

Start Date: _____ **End Date:** _____ **Renewable?** _____

Firmware Version _____ **Revision:** _____

OS/IOS Version _____ **Revision:** _____

Support Contact: _____

Contract Information/Password: _____

LAN/Internal IP		WAN/External IP		Security	
IP		IP		User Name:	
SN		SN			
GW		GW		Password:	
IP		IP			

Access Rules

Service name	Port #:	Protocol(s):	Access	Source IP:	Destination IP:

NAT/PAT

External IP address	Ports	Description	Internal IP	Ports

Network Passwords

Domain   Login: _____

Password: _____

Active Directory Restore   Login: _____

Password: _____

Virus Protection   Login: _____

Password: _____

Application logins

Backup Software   Login: _____

Password: _____

Hardware logins

Router - _____

Login: _____

Password: _____

Telnet Password: _____

Full Access Password: _____

Firewall - _____

Login: _____

Password: _____

Telnet Password: _____

Full Access Password: _____

Contracts, Warranties and License Information

Vendor	Type	Device	Start Date	Expiration

Software License & Install Key Information

Computer:		
Vendor	**Type**	**Install Key/Code**

Notes:

IP Schema

IP Standards for Usage

IP Address	Start	End	Description of Usage

Internal IP Scheme

Servers

Machine Name	IP Address	Def. GW	Subnet	External Outbound IP

External IP Scheme

External IP	Ports	Description	Internal IP	Ports

Key Device Information

Router

    Make and Model: _____

    S/N: _____

    External IP Address: _____

    Internal IP Address: _____

    Location: _____

    Warranty Info: _____

Firewall

    Make and Model: _____

    S/N: _____

    External IP Address: _____

    Internal IP Address: _____

    Location: _____

    Warranty Info: _____

Ethernet Switch1

    Make and Model: _____

    Type: _____

    S/N: _____

    External IP Address: _____

    Internal IP Address: _____

    Location: _____

    Internal IP Address: _____

    Warranty Info: _____

Ethernet Switch2

    Make and Model: _____

    Type: _____

    S/N: _____

    Location: _____

    Warranty Info: _____

Printer Information

Make and Model: _____

Serial Number: _____

Warranty/Support Contract#: _____

Start Date: _____ **End Date:** _____ **Renewable?** _____

Firmware Version _____ **Revision:** _____

Support Contact: _____

Contract Information/Password: _____

Management IP/URL: _____

Login: (User Name/Password) _____

Network IP: _____

Shared Name: _____

Host Server: _____

Driver Name: _____

Network Path To Install File: _____

Consumables		
Description	MFG PN	Preferred Vendor
Black toner		
Cyan		
Magenta		
Yellow		
Imaging Drum		

PDU INFORMATION

Make and Model: _____

Serial Number: _____

Location/Rack: _____

Warranty/Support Contract#: _____

Start Date: _____ End Date: _____ Renewable? _____

Firmware Version _____ Revision: _____

Support Contact: _____

Contract Information/Password: _____

Management IP/URL: _____

User Name: _____

Password:

Special Notes:

Ports	Description
1	
2	
3	
4	
5	
6	
7	
8	

KVM INFORMATION

Make and Model: _____ __ of __

Serial Number: _____

Location/Rack: _____

Warranty/Support Contract#: _____

Start Date: _____ End Date: _____ Renewable? _____

Firmware Version _____ Revision: _____

Support Contact: _____

Contract Information/Password:

Management IP/URL: _____	Cable set type/PN:
User Name: _____	
Password:	

Special Notes:

Ports	Description
1	
2	
3	
4	
5	
6	
7	
8	

Computer Details Form

Computer Name: _____

Vendor: _____   Chassis: _____

Serial Number: _____   Asset Tag: _____

Lease Expiration: _____

Warranty Info: _____

Operating System: _____   Service Pack: _____

Virus Protection: _____   Expiration: _____

Hardware Configuration:			
CPU:	Memory:	Video	Backup Device
# Hard Drives:	Network Card	Modem:	RAID Controller

Hard Drive:	Vol. Name:	Part. Size	Used Space:	Free Space:

Local Printers, Devices, Peripherals:

Application :	Key:

Notes:

PC Summary Form

Computer	Vendor	Serial #	Operating System	CPU	RAM	Disk

Page _____ OF _____

File and Print Shares

Network File Shares

Server	Share Name	Directory Path	Permissions

Network IP Printers

Server	Share Name	IP Address	Printer Type

Home Directory Information

Server	Share Name	Directory Path

Network Settings

WINS

Server Name:	
Item	**Description**
IP Address	
Purpose	
Replication Configuration	

DHCP

Server Name:	
Item	**Description**
IP Address	
Scope	
Exclusions	
Options	

DNS

Server Name:	
Item	**Description**
IP Address	
Forward Lookup Zones	
Forward Lookup Zone Type	
Reverse Lookup Zone	
Reverse Lookup Zone Type	
Manually configured hosts	

Local DNS Host Record Sheet

Domain Name: _____

Host/Node	Type (A, CName, MX)	IP address (Public)

Active Directory Domain Information

Item	Description
Active Directory Domain:	
NetBIOS Domain Name	
Domain Admin Account	
AD Restore Password	
Domain Controllers:	
Global Catalogue Servers:	
MS Exchange Server	

Active Directory Sites

Site Name:	Location	IP Range	Subnet

FSMO Roles

Role	Active Directory Location
Schema Master	
Domain Naming Master	
RID Master	
PDC Emulator	
Infrastructure Master	

Server Roles

Server Name	Roles in Network

IIS

Item	Description
Version	
InetPub Location	
Purpose	
Security	
Frontpage Extensions	

Routing and Remote Access

Item	Description
Remote Access Ports	
Remote Access Security	
Remote Access Policy Specs	
IP Assigned Via	
Routing Purpose	
NAT Configuration	

MS SQL Database Information Form

MS SQL SERVER INFORMATION			
Server:			
Product:		Version:	
Startup Parameters:			
Security:		Audit Level:	
Instance Name:			
SA User / PW			

Login Name	PW	Database assigned	Roles/Rights

DATABASES			
Name:		Compat. Level:	
DB File/Path			Size:
LOG File/Path			Size:
DATABASES			
Name:		Compat. Level:	
DB File/Path			Size:
LOG File/Path			Size:
DATABASES			
Name:		Compat. Level:	
DB File/Path			Size:
LOG File/Path			Size:

EMAIL Configuration

Overview

Microsoft Exchange Server Installation

Item	Data
Org name	
Site name	
Email Host Alias	
Computer name	
Service account	
Service account password	
Connectors	
Primary SMTP domain	
Additional SMTP Domains	
OWA URL	
Free Disk Space (%)	
Maintenance Schedule	

Component Location

Component	Location
Private information store (.edb)	
Private information store (.stm)	
Public information store (.edb)	
Public information store(.stm)	
Information store logs	
Directory service	
Directory service logs	
Message transfer agent	
Internet Mail Service files	
Key Management Server files	

Notes:

Backup Solution

Hardware

Hardware	Description
Tape Drive	
AutoLoader	
Driver version	
Updated/Firmware	

Software

Software	Description
Backup Software	
Version	
Responsibilities	
Day of Week	**Backup Job Details**
Monday	
Tuesday	
Wednesday	
Thursday	
Friday	
Saturday	
Sunday	

Tape Rotation

Sun	Mon	Tue	Wed	Thu	Fri	Sat

APPENDIX

Rest of page left blank intentionally

Login Script Details

Document Login Script contents and purpose/role of each.

Technical Notes/Change Log

Document notes and changes to the network

Date	Notes/Description
/ /	
/ /	
/ /	
/ /	
/ /	
/ /	
/ /	
/ /	
/ /	
/ /	
/ /	
/ /	
/ /	
/ /	
/ /	
/ /	
/ /	
/ /	
/ /	
/ /	

NOTES: